Film, Politics & Education

"This book provides an essential overview of the pedagogical rewards and challenges of using film in graduate and undergraduate classrooms. My own teaching at a school of public health will benefit greatly from the ideas in this important collection of essays."

Michael Yudell, Drexel University

"This is a wonderful book that should be read by everyone interested in good, joyful teaching. What is great about it is the way in which its contributors show just how effectively film can be used in the classroom by catalyzing discussion, bringing critical ideas to the fore, and enriching mass education."

Karen Anderson, York University

"Although often argued to be soft pedagogy, these authors present a convincing case for the use of film as a tool to assist learners in symbolic as well as literary analysis. This book is timely and sure to give voice to the necessity for expanding the employment of new pedagogical strategies."

Kassie Freeman, Southern University and A & M College System

Film, Politics,
& Education

PETER LANG
New York • Washington, D.C./Baltimore • Bern
Frankfurt am Main • Berlin • Brussels • Vienna • Oxford

Film, Politics, & Education

Cinematic Pedagogy Across the Disciplines

KELVIN SHAWN SEALEY, EDITOR

PETER LANG

New York • Washington, D.C./Baltimore • Bern
Frankfurt am Main • Berlin • Brussels • Vienna • Oxford

Library of Congress Cataloging-in-Publication Data

Film, politics, & education: cinematic pedagogy across the disciplines /
edited by Kelvin Shawn Sealey.
p. cm.
Includes bibliographical references and index.
1. Motion pictures in education—United States.
2. Teaching—Aids and devices.
I. Sealey, Kelvin Shawn. II. Title: Film, politics, and education.
LB1044.F452   371.33'523—dc22   2008000228
ISBN 978-0-8204-7882-1 (hardcover)
ISBN 978-0-8204-7881-4 (paperback)

Bibliographic information published by **Die Deutsche Bibliothek.**
Die Deutsche Bibliothek lists this publication in the "Deutsche
Nationalbibliografie"; detailed bibliographic data is available
on the Internet at http://dnb.ddb.de/.

Cover design by Joshua Hanson

The paper in this book meets the guidelines for permanence and durability
of the Committee on Production Guidelines for Book Longevity
of the Council of Library Resources.

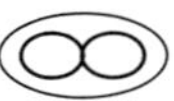

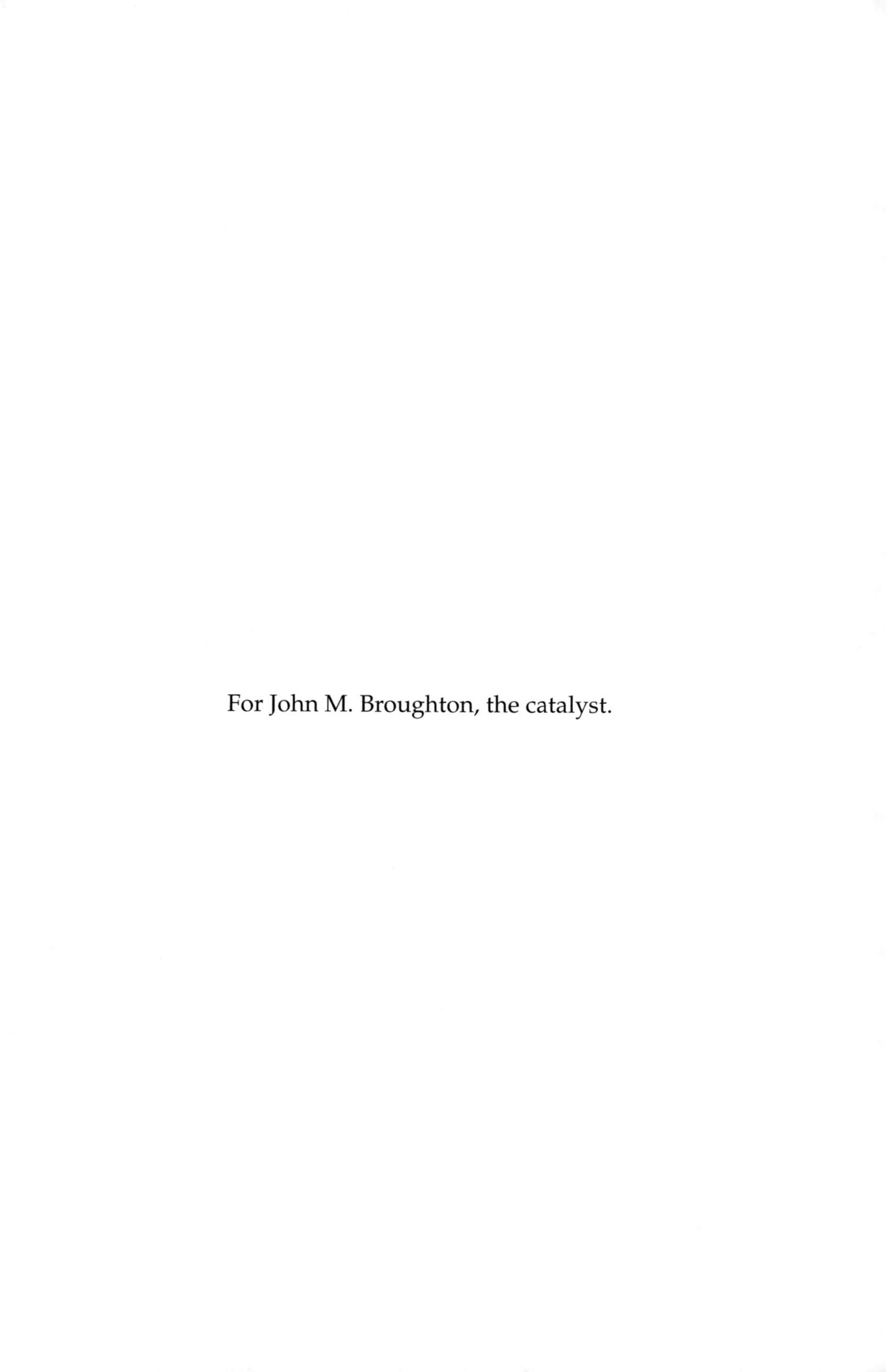

For John M. Broughton, the catalyst.

Contents

Acknowledgements

Grateful acknowledgement is hereby made to copyright owners for permission to use the following copyrighted material that did not fall under fair use guidelines:

Altered States of Vision: Film, Video and the Teaching of Architectural History (c) 1993 by Barry Bergdoll. All rights reserved. This essay originally appeared in Architecture on Screen, compiled and edited by the Program for Art on Film (Boston: G.K. Hall & Co., 1993). Reprinted with permission.

Teaching Positions: Difference, Pedagogy and the Power of Address, by Elizabeth Ellsworth (1997). New York: Teachers College Press, Teachers College, Columbia University. Chapter 1, pp. 21–36.

Film, Politics, and Education: Cinematic Pedagogy Across the Disciplines

KELVIN SHAWN SEALEY

Introduction

Considerable debate has occurred across much of the second half of the twentieth century concerning the value of cultural studies to the field of education generally, and within particular classrooms specifically. Debate continues to this day, suggesting an incomplete or inconsistent definition of "value" where utilization of pop cultural output is the measure, strangling attempts to generate useful new pedagogical tools within educational systems that are sorely in need of revision. Here in the early twenty-first century, with the clear ascendancy of techno-logically mediated pop cultural output as a dominating presence in youth culture, it would seem logical, if not imperative, that educational policy-makers, researchers, and theorists embrace curriculum design that recognizes this dominance while using it for its value as a teaching and learning tool.[1] From my perspective within the academy, and spe-cifically within a graduate school of education, I'm afraid that just the opposite may be true: those in positions of power within the education establishment who actively oppose the use of popular film, music, video games, comic books, videotapes, and other pop culture fragments as aids in the educational endeavor, still hold considerable sway.

This is no small charge, but I am led to level it as a result of my own teaching of graduate and undergraduate students in education for the past four years, a small fragment of time relative to many of my peers in the academy, but more than enough to gather the anecdotal and empirical evidence from students, teachers, and researchers reporting on the opposition educators face—from parents, principals, department heads, superintendents, and sometimes, if rarely, students themselves—to the use of pop cultural output in the contemporary classroom. This text grows out of my frustration with that situation, and my engagement with six classes of graduate and undergraduate students who chose to take my courses on the use of film in education. I hope, with this text, to reinforce in readers my belief in the imperative for popular culture output to be used in the teaching of young people, and for popular film in particular to become a more standard and accepted part of the educational arsenal.

My interest in the use of film in the classroom grows principally from my passion for education rather than my passion for film. While I share with my cinemaphilic colleagues a love for a good story rendered in the moving cinematic image, I am far more concerned about teachers facing unequal competition from popular film and music for the attention of the young people they are charged with educating. Given the ease and accessibility of DVDs, CDs, television, and now the Internet, each of which offers films of potent interest to school-aged children, the completion of teacher-assigned homework, the reading of literature, the repetitive practice and thought that we educators hope our students will engage in while not in our presence are less likely to happen spontaneously. There are far too many more exciting activities within arms' reach. In my scholarship and teaching practice, I concentrate on the use of film as a *supplement* to contemporary methods of teaching because I believe in the power of film to convey information critical to my students' understanding of important ideas. Film, to my mind, must not become a substitute for good teaching, but can be an aid to passionate and well-informed teaching. As a classroom tool, it can catalyze a valuable discussion, or display in visual form a critical idea that might remain too abstract or remote when encountered in discussion, literature, or debate. And film, given its potential to connect to our emotional center, and as a device for pleasure-seeking, for fantasy, or for the experience of alternative ways of thinking or being, can help teachers connect with their students along the important but often ignored dimension of joy.[2] I equate joyful learning in the classroom with good teaching; I equate good teaching with resourceful educators and engaged students. In contemporary Western culture, film can engage students in such a way as to advance a deliberate, pedagogically critical engagement with knowledge and with the world at large.

I have gone a long way toward advancing a broad argument in these first paragraphs without laying out critical definitions or backing my arguments with important historical and empirical references the reader may find of value. So, with that in mind, I'll begin at the beginning, again.

Film

Film, Politics, and Education brings together the work of eight educators from a variety of academic backgrounds who collectively agree on the wisdom of pedagogic interface between elements of popular culture and teaching/learning strategies in the classroom. Collectively, the authors represented here are specifically enamored with the power of film to transmit knowledge visually in a way that literary or oral transmission alone cannot, and with the depth, breadth, variety, and popularity of film as cause for its use in education. From my perspective, film represents a tool that educators can wield to advance any academic subject within any classroom. The reasons I advocate for its use grow from my observation of its power within the culture of the contemporary West, a power anchored in its ubiquity and cultural embrace. Film's clear visuality, the way it allows for the consumption of knowledge and ideas with the eye, its potential for touching our emotions, and, with the rise of technology in education, the growing ease of its use in the classroom, augers well for its pedagogical use.

For the last forty-five years, first a small, then a growing literature has tracked the use of film in the classroom. Although Bergdoll (1993), in this volume, points to the use of film in art and architecture classrooms as early as the 1920s and 1930s, instances in which undergraduate and graduate professional schools utilized advanced technology in narrowly focused elite environments, the history of film and education in the public school classroom tracks closely the evolution of technology easily accessible to the elementary school teacher. As early as 1937, Hoban, Hoban, and Zisman argued that various newly formed classifications of audiovisual materials allowed teachers to determine what audiovisual materials actually were, and then how best to use them within any given context, suggesting that audio and projection technology was finding its way into dialog about public classrooms in the first half of the twentieth century. At that time, even a field trip was considered a type of audiovisual experience; in today's jargon, this same trip might be called "experiential education," but the point is the same. Both student and teacher, at some remove from traditional classroom practice, engage a nontraditional teaching and learning paradigm, one which assumes that a variety of educational experiences best illustrates both the diversity of the world and the ability of various models of teaching and learning to be effective in passing on knowledge. Using film, as opposed to taking a field trip, required the teacher—or an assistant—to be conversant with the technology that allowed for the use of film. Today, of course, the DVD, the video recorder, and the computer are the projection/display devices of choice.

By the 1960s, with filmstrips and projected moving images finding their way into public classrooms, the contemporary basis for using film in the classroom can be said to have solidified, in no small part because of the ease of use and access to the technology for cinematic projection. Indeed, by the late 1950s, Lefranc (1959) could write in a UNESCO publication for the United Nations that "the place of the filmstrip in most school systems seems to be fairly well defined," though he also cautioned that

> ... the filmstrip takes a modest though useful place between material that is not screened or which can be screened with an episcope, and the cinema and television. (p. 13)

Though the subject of this text is the use of the moving image in education, I mention filmstrips here because, as Lefranc also points out, in the early years of films' use in the classroom, filmstrips often accompanied the film, with "each of the stills [serving] as a visual summary of a scene or sequence" (p. 24). The filmstrip thus updated the much longer use of still photography in the classroom, and was often used in conjunction with film as the moving image found a place in the same classrooms. Besides showing an interesting overlap in display technologies as used in the classroom, Lefranc also reveals how technology impacts the way teachers have chosen to use film, as well as the constraints and opportunities it has presented within the classroom.

By the 1970s, with the presence of film projectors growing in number within Western public schools, teachers found themselves confronted by school libraries that increasingly stocked educational films on which they could draw to enhance—or replace—lessons on a variety of subjects. Texts such as Amelio's (1971) *Film in the Classroom: Why Use It; How to Use It*, or Miller's (1979) *Films in the Classroom: A Practical Guide* set out the basic parameters for showing mainly educational films in schools. Katz's (1972) *A Curriculum in Film* is one of many texts of that time which broadened the theme of films' use in the classroom by considering the notion of visual literacy, the study of film as a subject in its own right, and by identifying the value that a number of films, both popular and instructional, might have in the classroom. As early as 1965, the National Council of Teachers of English published a text titled *The Motion Picture and the Teaching of English*, encouraging its members to consider how film might enhance the teaching of literature in the intermediate and high school classroom. Ross's (1970) edited text, *Film and the Liberal Arts*, reflected the depth to which the film had penetrated the liberal arts on American college campuses by the beginning of the 1970s, preparing that generation of teachers that finds itself ensconced in k-12 classrooms across the country today, as well as in positions of power in the educational establishment.

Politics

By the 1980s and 1990s, well into what many theorists have called the late modern or postmodern era, one in which the global saturation of societies by spectacular and technologically mediated mass entertainment reached new levels of pervasiveness, the call for new forms of visual literacy, the weight of mass culture on research in all fields of study, and the sheer volume of films released by Hollywood for the large and small screens made the use of film in the classroom almost impossible to ignore. That did not mean, however, that film was embraced at all levels of education or in all fields of educational endeavor. Indeed, while Denzin (1995) could point to the birth of the "cinematic society"[3] in the second half of the twentieth century, we have yet to fully embrace the use of film as an important component of teaching and learning. This is where I believe "politics" enters the equation of film in the classroom.

Without entering into the long and contentious debate over the direction that the so-called culture wars have taken in the last twenty years, we need not be reminded too often that our society—indeed, all societies—is a formation of blocks of power, formal and informal contestations of legitimacy and rights, fragments and justifications of truth and history. With the history of cultural studies firmly rooted in a Marxist vision of the world, a vision that contests the right of capital to control labor and resources, and that seeks to understand where, how, and by what means power is exercised over the masses in all societies, we who seek to use elements of popular culture in the classroom confront the history of this contestation. Further, the intellectual might of the Frankfurt School[4] theorists, whose long argument against the value of mass culture or pop culture artifacts weighs heavily upon the notion of film in the classroom, and thus upon the educator who seeks to conflate high culture and low, intrudes in many cases. In short, the use of film as a component of popular culture falls on the wrong side of contemporary history, and as a result, fights an uphill battle in recognition and pedagogical value within systems of educational power.

I have used the word "politics" in the title of this text, and in the title of my course of the same name, to identify elements of the environment that teachers may face when seeking to use film in the classroom. If, as I argue, the prevailing opinion within the elite establishment of educational researchers and policy makers is that advanced by the Frankfurt School, then some educators will find it difficult if not impossible to properly advance a teaching and learning strategy that utilizes popular film within the contemporary classroom. Politics, from the perspective of the teacher, can take the form of disciplinary questions, active dissuasion on the part of superiors, expressed concern and/or consternation on the part of parents or colleagues, or downright hostility from any individual quarter. Despite the depth of literature that addresses the importance of cultivating visual literacy, or which advances a positive notion of engagement with popular culture in many individual fields of study, or which recognizes the value popular film can have in a classroom environment, a political dimension that is antithetical to the cinematic presence in the classroom is always a possibility. Indeed, though I write these words while sitting in a large northeastern U.S. city, where many of my students work as teachers, I have met many who hail from much smaller regions of the country where traditional teaching does not include the use of popular film. It remains important, therefore, to continue to beat the drum of education and cultural studies generally, and film and education specifically, if we are to broaden the diversity of teaching styles to include some of what pop culture is producing for general consumption.

Education

In this text, education is broadly defined. Although most of my students teach pre-k through twelfth-grade public school curricula, my film and education methods can be used outside of these boundaries, in post-secondary and graduate education, professional education, adult and lifelong education, and every field taught in the technical or liberal arts. I have coined the term *cinematic education* to refer to teaching and learning infused with the moving image. Cinematic education does not refer exclusively to the projection of feature films on a screen in a classroom for 120 minutes, after which discussion is held about the contents of said film. This method is best left to film educators, though the work of film educators can rightfully be called, by my definition, cinematic education as well. In my own work, I have been far more interested in finding ways of using "pieces" of film to allow my students to enter into discussion and debate with the clarity of a visual image as the catalyst. Rarely do I show a film in its entirety during a class period. I find it better to assign the watching of film as an at-home task well before or after formal class time.

Aesthetically and philosophically, I am more concerned with small visual elements in film, with scenes, scenery, and architecture cinematically rendered; with colors and sound, with title sequences and flashes of light, with the races, genders, sexual orientations, religions, and ethnicities of the characters as they appear before me on screen. These "pieces" of film, shown in small bits, with the classroom lights off or on, with the sound muted or loud, in regular, fast, or slow motion, are the elements of cinematic education, the *vocabulary* of a cinematic pedagogy. Combined with each educator's individual pedagogical style, and with an academic intention behind a given lesson plan, the cinematic can add visual and intellectual rigor unparalleled by other modes of expression. Expanding Ellsworth's notion of "mode of address," film speaks to us in a way that lectures, readings, and argumentative orality cannot. This is, to my mind, the value of cinematic education in today's classroom.

Examples of Cinematic Education

To better illustrate the point I am trying to make, I will endeavor to describe two moments of teaching and learning that highlighted for me the dynamic nature of using film in the classroom. Each of these examples is taken from one of the six classes in film and education I have taught over the last four years, and highlighted for me the value of training teachers to utilize film in their respective classes. In both cases, I did not use a film scene to point to a topic specific to the fields in which my students taught, but merely opened an intellectual space in which film might act as a catalyst for discussion on whatever topic emerged from the viewing of that piece of film.

The first example draws on the Chinese film *Crouching Tiger Hidden Dragon* (motion picture) (Lee, 2000). Midway through the movie, the two main characters—a man and a woman—are involved in a chase scene through a forest, the woman, in this case, chasing the man. The Hollywood magic that imbues this film allows characters to fly through the air as if weightless, and thus allows them to skip over bodies of water, walk upright into the branches of trees while defying gravity, and otherwise perform acrobatic feats generally impossible for ordinary human beings. The scene I used lasts approximately two minutes on screen.

I chose to show this chase scene in three separate modes: with the sound turned off, so that viewers could only guess at the dialog being used; with the sound on, but only after discussion of the scene viewed with the sound off; and finally, with the sound on, but with the screen facing the classroom wall, such that all one could hear was the sound track, which in this case included both dialog and music.

After the first two-minute viewing, with the sound turned off, I asked students to write what they believed the characters were saying based on what they had seen them doing in the scene. The ensuing discussion highlighted the beauty of the cinematography, the way the director chose to highlight certain aspects of the attractive features of the male or female characters, how the color of the landscape, which was green, gave the scene a natural feeling even though the characters were behaving in a way physically unnatural for humans. There were at least six or seven different viewpoints related to the class by students, and each viewpoint had validity as a topic of discussion within my classroom. We then watched the scene again, this time with sound.

Some of my students had seen this film before class, and therefore understood the context in which the scene took place within the film. For my purposes, this was unimportant. Some of those seeing the film for the first time, upon hearing the dialog coupled with the scene, were surprised at the types of sounds associated with the action. In several cases, points of the action did not appear to call for specific sounds—a grunt, for instance, or a laugh—that the film did, in fact, contain. So we discovered that discontinuities between sounds and images were possible, and that created opportunity for a discussion on the realms of sound and activity. Several art teachers in the room found utility in this new concept—using film to highlight disjunctures between action and sound in a film—for activities they would create in their own class-rooms. Other students pointed to the way sound was used to create an inequality between the male and the female characters, an inequality that matched some of what was visible in the scene on its first view-ing. So, in this case, sound accented the disjuncture in the characters' relative power. This point, in turn, led to discussion about how men and women in society are portrayed in film, magazines, television, and other visual media as weaker than men even if their skills, or skill sets, are relatively even.

The final use of this clip, listening to the soundtrack without seeing the television screen, provided a different terrain for the imagination of my students. Now, having seen the scene in two different contexts, would listening rather than seeing and listening together provide yet another dimension of analysis?

After listening to the scene, several students found themselves thinking of other ways the director (or director of photography) might have shot the scene while conveying the same message about the characters. Others considered how little about the sound track would lead one to believe that the scene took place within the branches of trees deep in a forest, which is the actual location in which the scene takes place. Still others pointed out that the music, together with the dialog, did more than either of them—music or dialog—could have accomplished alone, thereby highlighting the various dimensions sound can take within the context of a contemporary film.

When I asked students to consider how this single scene could be used in the context of their respective fields, much like the art student had mentioned her recognition of disjunctures between sound and action, there were many ideas. A high school physics teacher suggested that on watching this scene, she could envision asking students to enumerate the physical theories that the characters broke in order for the scene to take place in the way that it did. A civics teacher made mention of the environment—the lush, green forest in which the scene plays out—and suggested that upon watching this scene in his classroom a conversation might ensue which might point to the value of certain conservation measures which would allow forests like that witnessed in the film to survive on earth for another thousand years or more. Indeed, that same civics classroom could also consider how the scene would look if conservation measures are not taken in this century. A junior high school English teacher considered that her students might be asked to write the dialog for each character after watching the scene without sound, and in so doing, cultivate an affinity for understanding dialogical address between characters in a screenplay as opposed to that found in a novel or stage play. And finally, an elementary school art teacher found the dominating color scheme—forest green—a wonderful element on which to build a lesson on color: what it can mean, how it can be witnessed, what the natural earth gives us to dwell upon, and how color is important in conveying certain ideas to a viewer.

I have described this sequence of activity and discussion in some depth to drive home the diversity of viewpoints, fields of study, age groups, professions, and ideologies that a single two-minute scene can be used to underscore, using the simplest of technologies (tv/vcr) and one of the most powerful elements of popular culture: film. In my classes in cinematic education, I screen dozens of films, some for as little as five seconds, extracting minutiae that some might find unusual, but which, in many cases, leads to discussions about possibilities few in the room had before attending this class. This is not a pat on the back; indeed, I have always come from instances of these classes having learned some-thing I didn't know before I went in. This, to my mind, is the nature of teaching and learning when both student and teacher are in a position to be recognized as both. What I do hope I've demonstrated is the breadth of uses to which film—small segments of film—can be put in a variety of subjects across all age groups. It remains only for you, the teacher, to recognize moving pictures as malleable instances of activity capable of being mapped to your individual ideas and expressions, all for the ben-efit of enlivening a sequence of intellectual exchanges in your classroom that may allow both you and your students to blossom in ways you can now only imagine.

I wish to mention another example of the type of discussion that can arise with the use of film in the classroom. In this case, the discussion was around the film *Kill Bill Vol. II* (motion picture) (Tarantino 2004) and the level of violence the director Quentin Tarantino associated with his characters.[5] My class, in this instance, was comprised of graduate edu-cation students, most of whom were women; indeed, all but one student were female. The subject of gendered violence arose: to what extent did Tarantino place women in a position to violently confront one another in ways that many people associate with men? In this case, two of the main female characters—Uma Thurman and Daryl Hannah—engage in a scene of swordplay, with one violently killing the other in a death match we have seen acted by male characters tens of thousands of times in the movies. But in this case, two attractive, blond women were having a go at each other with swords.

Most of my students raised the issue of Tarantino himself, and considered this scene a proper extension of his bloody cinematic corpus, regardless of the character's gender. But one student remarked on the value of the scene for girls and women, who often operate in a world where friends and enemies wear the same smile. She made mention of her own life, and the number of times when girls she believed were her friends—in school, in the neighborhood, and so on—often turned out to be working, in some way, against her. In the fight scene from *Kill Bill Vol. II*, the fact that each woman knew the other was an enemy, and was prepared to have it out with her to settle the score, was seen as a step above the backbiting, hypocritical activity my student had witnessed in her own life. Several other students in the room agreed wholeheartedly.

As a male, and as the instructor, I must admit that I was a little taken aback. I had never heard an argument like this before, but I found it fascinating in the context of a class on film and education. But regardless of your view toward this student's self-revelation, it is this type of serendipity that constantly arises when filmic displays are taken out of their traditional context and placed side by side with ideas, sounds, books, exams, photographs, pencils, paint, and the many other tools for teaching and learning. By raising issues of gender violence in a small piece of popular film, a conversation opened on the dynamics of female-female relations generally, one that my students thought might be very useful in a number of ways. While it is important to recognize that certain scenes of violence and sexual activity—overt or implied—should be kept out of many classrooms, there are means by which the utility of otherwise unnoticed scenes may be broadened by the creative use of film in the classroom.

Chapters

The seven educators besides myself who address the cinematic as a valuable aspect of contemporary education do so from a number of perspectives, representing the sheer diversity of styles, fields, and intellectual currents with which the cinematic can be blended in order to teach. In *Chapter 1*, John Broughton gives us a picture of the history behind the use of film in the classroom, drawing upon both philosophical theories and practical classroom experience.

Taking issue with arguments made by scholar Nadine Dolby in an influential *Harvard Education Review* article, Annette Bickford uses *Chapter 2* to contest the wholesale acceptance of popular culture output as inherently democratic, pointing out that a more nuanced view of all cultural output—popular or elite—should frame any discussion of democracy and its practice in the West.

Chapter 3 draws on the interdisciplinary work of Elizabeth Ellsworth to unfold the notion of "mode of address," the give and take between film and audience in which each member of that audience is identified by the film being viewed. As a concept anchored in film studies, Ellsworth nevertheless marks its importance as a point of intellectual geography, allowing astute users of the cinematic to wrestle with yet another nuance film brings to the pedagogical arena.

In *Chapter 4*, Barry Bergdoll combines his experience as an instructor of art history and architecture with the cinematic to reveal the history of these two fields and their encounter with film, and his own observation of how history, technology, and philosophy have had an impact on the teaching of architectural history. While architecture and film may not seem a natural alliance, Bergdoll gives sound reason why the two have not only had a pleasant alliance across the twentieth century, but also why this alliance might indeed be growing deeper here in the twenty-first century.

Chapter 5, by human rights educator Peter Lucas, considers how film has "seeded" peace education in Brazil, allowing educators to raise difficult subjects within an emotionally scorched environment with the use of film.

In Chapter 6, Chyng Sun takes the Gramscian concept of hegemony and marries it to Disney's film *The Lion King* (motion picture) (Allers & Minkoff 1994), producing an insightful take on the popular animated film. While a separate series of texts could be devoted to animated film and education, Sun's work represents an important instance of mapping contemporary cultural theory to popular cinematic fare in ways that both enlighten us to the density of animated film and excavate tissue of cultural and intellectual value from this fascinating artifact of modern life.

The final chapter, rendered in dialogical style, is located in the text as an Afterward. Following an earlier unfinished public conversation I held with scholar and cultural critic bell hooks at Columbia University in the fall of 2003, she and I reexamine her beliefs about the importance of film in popular culture generally and in education specifically. Having followed bell's work on film across several decades, it was good to confirm that hooks still believes in the power of film to push us toward greater critical thinking, particularly in light of the reign of less activist cinematic work than has been produced by Hollywood in the 1960s and 1970s. bell hooks reminds us of the leveling power of film, its ability to reach both into the ivory tower and out to the people on the street, bridging divides of class, religion, education, and power in a way that few elements in Western culture can so naturally achieve.

Conclusion

I mentioned earlier in this introduction that the use of film in the classroom can in no way become a substitute for good teaching, and it is worth mentioning here again. Dedicated teachers, given the resources they require, combined with a small classroom of motivated students eager to learn, has become the ideal for parents, teachers, and those who would hire them to teach. However, those of us who has recently engaged children in classrooms across the age spectrum, in all parts of the country, in multiple fields of learning, are certain that much needs to be done to aid the Western system of education before we collectively achieve the ideal everywhere.

What this text posits is that, given the tremendous power of popular culture output, with its visceral connection to both pleasure seeking and mass activity, the educational establishment might be well served to consider how film can enliven, diversify, deepen, enrich, and legitimate mass education for a large swath of the young public. Further, in postsecondary education, professional graduate education, and life-long education being considered by our increasingly older, re-training population, models of curriculum-design that bring the cinematic into the pedagogical fold can be a welcome and necessary update to models of teaching that are a century old or more.

As this text shows in academic prose by the diversity of its chapters, scholars are increasingly considering the benefits of a cinematic education paradigm, one that advances cinematic education as a valuable conceptual tool in the arsenal of educators across multiple fields of endeavor. At Teachers College, Columbia University, John Broughton and I work within *FERA—The Film & Education Research Academy*—to catalog the myriad ways film can add positively to the teaching experience for both student and teacher.[6] This research, along with that conducted by dozens of our colleagues worldwide, brings promise to those who look forward to a time when cinematic elements of popular culture enliven the admixture of pedagogy in public and private classrooms to a much greater extent than they do today.

Notes

1. By pop cultural output, I am referring to those creations of what Adorno (1991) called the "culture industry" that include television shows, radio programs, popular film, popular recorded music, comic books, video games, and other forms of mass entertainment. I should also point out that competing definitions of mass culture and popular culture militate against these terms being used interchangeably in this text. For examples of these competing definitions, see page 3 in Alvermann, Moon and Haygood (1999), and Chapter 1 in Strinati's (1995) "An Introduction to Theories of Popular Culture."
2. Alvermann, Moon, and Hagood (1999, p. 31) refer to the "politics of pleasure" as a vital concern of which educators must be aware when venturing onto the cultural terrain of young people in order to use it to teach.
3. Denzin was quoting Hitchcock, who suggested that the cinematic society was "that twentieth century social formation that knows itself through the cinematic apparatus." See Denzin (1999, p. 1).
4. Explanations of the Frankfurt School theorists and theories can be found in numerous sources, but for a succinct definition and overview, see Edgar and Sedgwick (1999).

5. Given their subject matter, most Tarantino films are best used, if at all, in class-rooms of adults rather than young people of high school age or below.

6. See http://www.filmandeducation.org. Those wishing to contribute to the research of the Academy, or merely wishing to be in contact, should e-mail either John Broughton or myself at jmb61@columbia.edu (John) or kss2008@columbia.edu (Kelvin).

References

Adorno, T. (1991). *The Culture Industry*. London: Routledge.

Allers, R. & Minkoff, R. (Directors) (1994). *The Lion King* [motion picture]. New York: Disney Motion Pictures.

Alvermann, D. E., Jennifer, S. M., & Hagood, M. C. (1999). *Popular Culture in the Classroom: Teaching and Researching Critical Media Literacy*. Chicago: National Reading Conference.

Amelio, R. J. (1971). *Film in the Classroom: Why Use It; How to Use It*. Ohio: Pflaum/Standard.

Bergdoll, B. (1993). Altered States of Vision: Film, Video, and the Teaching of Architectural History, in N. Covert (ed.) *Architecture on Screen: Films and Videos on Architecture, Landscape Architecture, Historic Preservation, City and Regional Planning*. New York: Metropolitan Museum of Art and the J. Paul Getty Trust.

Denzin, N. (1995). *The Cinematic Society: The Voyeur's Gaze*. London: Sage Publications.

Edgar, A. & Sedgwick, P. (1999). *Cultural Theory: The Key Concepts*. London: Routledge.

Hoban, C. F., Hoban, C. F. Jr., & Zisman, S. B. (1937). *Visualizing the Curriculum*. New York: Cordon Company.

Katz, J. (1972). *A Curriculum in Film*. Toronto: Ontario Institute for Studies in Education.

Lee, A. (Director) (2000). *Crouching Tiger, Hidden Dragon* [motion picture]. New York: Sony Pictures Entertainment.

Lefranc, R. (1959). Use of Filmstrips, in *Filmstrips: Use, Evaluation and Production*. Brussels: UNESCO.

Miller, H. (1979). *Films in the Classroom: A Practical Guide*. New Jersey: Scarecrow Press.

National Council of Teachers of English. (1965). *The Motion Picture and the Teaching of English*. New York: Appleton-Century-Crofts.

Ross, T. J. (ed.) (1970). *Film and the Liberal Arts*. New York: Holt, Reinhart & Winston.

Strinati, D. (1995). *An Introduction to Theories of Popular Culture*. London: Routledge.

Tarantino, Q. (Director) (2004). *Kill Bill Vol. II* [motion picture]. United States: Miramax Films.

Chapter One

Inconvenient Feet: How Youth and Popular Culture Meet Resistance in Education

JOHN BROUGHTON[1]

Tap versus Chant: "Low" Culture and Its Antithesis

The 2007 Academy Awards ceremony was perhaps most noted for the Oscar won by Vice President Al Gore's eco-documentary *An Inconvenient Truth*. A great deal of (well-deserved) hoo-ha was made about this compelling expression of concern, and about its Cassandrian theme song "I Need to Wake Up," delivered with suitable urgency by Melissa Etheridge—a bit of an edgy social figure herself.

In contrast, the Oscar awarded to George Miller's enormously successful *Happy Feet*, as best full-length animated feature, went almost unnoticed, despite the fact that it offered a similar moral lesson in the ecology of survival.

In *Happy Feet*, the dramatic climax down under in the Antarctic community of Emperor penguins, threatened with man-made starvation, is a standoff between two separate factions. The popular tap dancing group of the hero, "Mumble," featuring a merry band of irreverent homosocial acolytes from south of the border, is cavorting bravely but gleefully down below. In contrast, the classically trained vocal choir of stern, entrenched elders (trained by the traditionalist voice teacher Mrs Astrakhan), perch on the higher reaches of the ice floe, chanting sonorously. Youth and recency confront maturity and history, in a battle of sounds, the disruptive syncopations struggling against the tidal current of flowing, formal harmonies.

The camera suggestively scans the perpendicular spatial arrangement, revealing the visual structure of power.[2] The unquestioned authority of the more spiritual sophisticates establishes itself at the apex, headed by a dour and rigid Scotsman, part-penguin, part-vulture in countenance; the choristers assume the synchronized, transported sway of an angelic host. The more physical, popular counterculture, with its non-Eurocentric taint of ethnic diversity is headed by a "learning disabled" exile or refugee figure, whose impulsive hoofer talents had failed to submit to the rigors of the standardized curriculum; his motley crew is relegated to ground level.

As the International Movie Database phrases it in their plot summary, "the deeply conformist leadership of the colony fearfully blames the young penguin's unorthodox ways for the lean fishing that threatens them all," showing how the vertical spatial order translates into a commanding moral order, with the elders arrogating to themselves unquestionable rectitude and contemptuously blaming the victim-other and his illegal immigrant friends.

Even though children's culture has been known to oversimplify, and despite the fact that Hollywood, even in its animated films, revels in the stereotype, Miller's *Happy Feet* alerts us to the fact that three groups of cultural tensions—between lower and higher, body and mind, foot and mouth, gestural and verbal; between youth and age, play and work, entertainment and knowledge, pleasure and control; and between open and closed, innovation and tradition, unfamiliar and familiar, curiosity and complacency, the fresh and the stuffy—tend to align themselves in a political struggle that we experience as both endemic to late modern society and the key to its survival. Moreover, this particular film suggests that the struggle in question is a narrative form worth dwelling upon reflectively at the same time that it is poignant and hugely amusing.

For our present purposes, *Happy Feet* is of particular interest because it depicts education—in the family, in school, in a supplementary after-school context, and through multicultural travel—as playing a major role not only in the resolution of cultural conflict but also in its generation. In addition, it is a dramatic case study of a child with the social stigma of a speech impediment who turns his disability into a talent and eventually uses it to teach not only his own community but also the human species the error of their ways.

The Aversion to Popular Culture in Schools

Today, the only modernism worthy of the name is antimodern modernism. (Kundera, 2007, p. 35)

Media educator Terrence Ross (2004–2005) bemoans the "disinclination to take media seriously" because of their being a "peripheral diversion," characterized by a "lack of signification" (p. 657). Although he is one of those who do take media seriously, even he admits to worrying that most youth fare is "junk food" (ibid.). In the United Kingdom, Education Secretary John Patten used classical alliteration and ad hominem to make this same equation between popular culture and supersizing in the classroom: "They'd give us Chaucer with chips, Milton with mayonnaise. Mr. Chairman, I want William Shakespeare in our classrooms, not Ronald McDonald" (Buckingham & Sefton-Green, 1994, p. 1).[3]

Antipathy to the popular is certainly not confined to education, nor is it particularly new. Its roots (the proximal ones, at least) could be traced to the erstwhile battle over the vulgarity of "kitsch" that Kundera (2007) describes as "the syrupy dregs of the romantic period," following Musil's "bread drenched in perfume" (p. 34), but which nevertheless was the dominant style in much of nineteenth-century continental Europe. In the history of kitsch, our own generation could lay claim to a relatively new phase: the instrumental use of normative education to draw the line that excludes the vulgar and challenges its claim to be included as part of the culture that schooling must admit.

The contemporary does not fit well into the time scheme of institutionalized pedagogy, which thrives on its reputation for sobriety and considered judgment, elevating permanence above transience by dismissing the "cultural present" in favor of the "canonized past," as Carmen Luke (1997, p. 21) puts it. As though assuming a crude socio-biological imperative—with survival of the fittest serving to weed out the trivial—institutionalization is taken as proof of legitimacy. Schooling is constrained accordingly: for example, past New York State Commissioner of Education Thomas Sobol (2006) defines "cultural education" as "education through libraries, museums, archives, and historical societies" (p. 11).

As Hall and Whannel (1964) and Gans (1999) have pointed out, there are a number of fronts on which the battle against popular culture has been fought. These could all be seen as representing conflicted areas in the broader terrain of modernism, sensitive spots in its hegemonic carapace. The major issues around which the struggle has been engaged are entertainment, the domestic environment, literature, textuality, immorality, commercialism, and immaturity.

Entertainment

(S)tudents learn to separate popular culture and "real education" at an early age. To most students, one exists in the realm of pleasure and the other in the realm of "sanctioned knowledge." (Tavin, 2000, p. 196)

First and foremost, popular culture has become suspect because of its entertaining character. Because of their casual, optional, and idiosyncratic nature, leisure pastimes clearly do not and cannot occupy, exercise, and develop consciousness in the way that rigorous formal instruction at the hands of professionally prepared teachers can. There is a quality of unbridled impulse to entertainment, what March (2005–2006) has called "instant media gratification" (p. 14). This excess, which Bataille (1985) called "expenditure," exceeds the functional requirements for consistent societal utility, exchange value, and system equilibrium. Hence, entertainment always threatens to cross some behavioral boundary, to disrupt or deracinate social order: modern adults live in fear "that the children are out of control and that media are a major culprit" (Ross, 2004–2005, p. 658).

That this is not an entirely new condition we are reminded by Plato:

> In the *Republic*, describing the ideal state, Plato already excludes popular music. Only the harp and Apollo's lyre would be permitted in towns because their harmony alone creates "the strain of necessity and the strain of freedom, the strain of the unfortunate and the strain of the fortunate, the strain of courage and the strain of temperance which befit the citizen." City-dwellers panicked before Pan's flute and its power to awaken the instincts. Only "the shepherds may play [Pan's] pipes and they only in the country." (Illich, 2002/1970, p. 107)

For Plato, it is the absence of moderation and balance in the regime of impulse that makes popular music so disruptive of urban life. So much so, that censorship of pop follows logically.

The lapse of temperance, the vertigo of the irrational, is feared on the political left as well—witness Adorno's (1981–1982) specific warning about the dangers of film: "The liberated film would have to wrest its *a priori* collectivity from the mechanisms of unconscious and irrational influence" (pp. 203–204). As Storey (2003, 2006) and Strinati (2004), among others, have pointed out, post-Marxists share their ambivalence about pop culture with cultural conservatives, and are equally as keen to expose and ridicule "kitsch," although for rather different reasons. The Frankfurt School as a whole was deeply concerned about the parallels between American popular culture and German fascism, hence their resort to the high modernist avant garde as an antidote.

The antipathy to pop is democratically distributed across the political spectrum; so much so that one finds it even among postmodernists. For example, the semiotic post-structuralist Jean Baudrillard (1990) argues against media culture on account of its mechanized quality and its lack of rhetorical sophistication:

> (I)t is useless and absurd to compare and contrast the merits of High Culture and Mass-Mediated Culture. The former has a complex "syntax," while the latter is a combinatory of elements always dissociable in terms of stimulus/ response and question/answer. This schema is most vividly illustrated by radio game shows. ... [C]onsumers are constantly solicited, "quizzed," and

summoned to respond, … a response that engages the individual in the collective ritual of consumption. (p. 69)

To this concern with a rational social life, liberal critics, such as Gitlin (1996), have added a psycho-pedagogical objection, that popular culture is not just marginal, trivial, or disruptive, it actually dulls consciousness: "[T]he vast entertainment machine is, among other things, an industry for numbing" (p. 65). Often, this critique of cultural numbing, made popular by Gitlin's colleague, the ego-psychologist Robert Lifton (1967), is linked to the "escapist" view of popular culture, as in a recent interview by David Thomson:

> You can't deny that cinema is a wonderful tool for expression, but there's a tendency for the medium to promote a world that's detached from reality. … I think that film can distance people from dealing with the world around them. … The last election in this country seemed to suggest that many people had given up fact for fantasy. I'm not sure that decades spent in the dark didn't contribute to that somewhat. (Fear, 2005, p. 85)

In educational terms, it is the impact on intelligence that is feared:

> For decades we've worked under the assumption that mass culture follows a steadily declining path toward lowest common denominator standards, presumably because the "masses" want dumb, simple pleasures and big media companies want to give the masses what they want. (Johnson, 2005, p. 9)

There is "a suspicion of entertainment *per se*, on the grounds that it necessarily represents a 'dumbing down'" (Buckingham & Scanlon, 2003, p. 111). The critique of popularization and the intellectual regression it fosters is often linked with accounts that attribute the retrograde consequences to hypnotic or narcotic effects. According to this view, not only are media seen derogatorily as all "consumed" (in contrast to, say, fine art, which is "appreciated"), but also as "all-consuming," addictive—as in "amusing ourselves to death" (Postman, 1986) or the "plug-in drug" (Winn, 1977).

Despite this array of critiques, there is a growing consensus that entertainment can be and often is educational. As Johnson (2005) concludes, "the most debased forms of mass diversion—video games and violent television dramas and juvenile sitcoms—turn out to be nutritional after all" (p. 9). In fact, in some settings for certain issues, entertainment-education may even be demonstrably superior as a pedagogical approach (Singhal & Rogers, 1999; Singhal, Cody, Rogers, & Sabido, 2003; Gee, 2003; Johnson, 2005). Arguably the most detailed piece of research on this issue is by Kelvin Sealey (2006).

Our extracurricular time may on occasion be less complex, less serious, or less demanding than our work life. But leisure resists trivialization. Entertainment "is not simply fluff that can be dismissed as irrelevant and insignificant; on the contrary, it has the capacity to intervene in the critical civic issues and to shape public opinion" (Dolby, 2003, p. 259). Carmen Luke (1997) and Nicholas Mirzoeff (1999) have documented a range of ways in which such issues arise within popular culture. In addition, Dolby points out that there is a more personal and relational quality to popular culture:

> It often serves as both a social "glue" and a social divider: friendships solidify around a shared love for a particular band, music video, or television show, and being outside of the currents of the popular can lead to social isolation. (ibid.)

Positive findings on education-entertainment echo what developmental psychologists have found regarding the importance of play for learning. Early anecdotal accounts, such as those of Piaget and Vygotsky, have since been backed up by more systematic empirical studies, such as those of Sutton-Smith (1980, 2001/1997) and colleagues (Pellegrini, 1995). The most important aspect turns out to be the fantasy component, not the "adaptive" play that is little more than a functional rehearsal for work.

Drawing on the notion of the "counterfactual conditional" developed by Nelson Goodman at Harvard's "Project Zero," Jerome Bruner (1987, 1991) has shown how vital the young person's experience of the "subjunctive" is—that possible, potential, imaginable yet not real condition, which fantasy play is ideally suited to foster—and how frequently in education it is eclipsed by "paradigmatic" thought that quashes metaphor, narrative, and the imaginary. It is precisely in this "as if" transitional zone that Winnicott (1970) finds the distinction between self and other is forged, with ludic, symbolic culture playing the major mediating role. Hence, perhaps the function of popular culture that Dolby identifies, as both social glue and social divider.

Home

I shall not escape the fate of all other boys. I shall be sent to school and I shall be made to study either by love or by force. To tell you in confidence, I have no wish to learn; it is much more amusing to run after butterflies, or to climb trees and to take the young birds out of their nests. (Collodi, 1968/1880, p. 26)

The opposition to the idea of entertainment as educative can be seen as an attempt to draw a firmer line between school and home. There is certainly evidence of a progressive blurring of the boundary between the two, and of the growing role of the family in learning (Buckingham & Scanlon, 2003). These authors see a useful gender division of labor in the home between women, who prefer recreational books, and men, who tend to exercise their relative expertise on computers. But they also note that the teachable moments in the family are not always desirable; these may reflect escalating demands within the schools that spill over into the home, depleting shared leisure time and turning the domestic environment into a satellite production site for accumulating educational capital (cf. Kovel, 1978). If anything, parents resist the professionalization of the home and the pressure to be recruited into the (unpaid) workforce of ancillary teachers.

Moreover, the leisure-time activities that promote spontaneous learning are often not appreciated by formal educators:

> [M]uch of the difficulty here stems from the problem of what we count as learning in the first place. Much of the learning and teaching that goes on in homes and families is not recognized by schools. (Buckingham & Scanlon, 2003, p. 191)

Even in early education, learning is typically construed vocationally and bureaucratically, that is, as a form of work that will contribute, directly or indirectly, to eventual employability (Apple, 2006; Kanter, 1972). Such vocationalism flies in the face of children's experience of their environment:

> Needless to say, perhaps, there is no recognition whatsoever ... that young children already live in a commercially based culture. ... Learning is a form of "work" that seems to proceed in ignorance of much of young children's everyday lives and cultural experiences. (Buckingham & Scanlon, 2003, p. 81)

Teachers already rely on the extensive foreknowledge of subject matter that their young proteges bring with them from this everyday cultural context. For example, how would it be possible for elementary teachers to conduct an in-class discussion of prehistory (especially the Triassic, Jurassic, and Cretaceous periods) without confronting and engaging the intense and complex culture of dinosaurs, in which children are already immersed—often in a highly participatory way (Gould, 1993).

What is more, scientific discourse in schools, despite presenting itself as objective and autonomous, frequently borrows from the language of the media. For example, elementary school texts on dinosaurs orient to films like the *Jurassic Park* series, adopting the metaphors and plot lines of horror and crime genres developed in that franchise (Buckingham & Scanlon, 2003). Paradoxically, and in a deconstructive manner, education is already suffused with popular media. The same authors point out the huge impact on youth consciousness of the *Star Wars* series, which, we should add, in the late 1970s and early 1980s played a major historical role in renewing curiosity about the universe, space travel, astronomy, and astrophysics.

Thus it is not always the case that educators need to recognize the value of popular culture outside the curriculum and then transform their pedagogy so as to accommodate it in some way. Rather, perhaps they should start by acknowledging and examining their own dependence on the popular, already embodied in prevailing texts and practices.

What we have learned from adult education is that just because we value our schools does not mean that we should ignore the fact that much of the needed learning context is already available in the way that the rest of our lives is situated:

> The point of education should not be to inculcate a body of knowledge, but to develop capabilities, ... to take initiative and to work creatively and collaboratively. The most important capability, and the one which traditional education is worst at creating is the ability and yearning to carry on learning. Too much schooling kills off a desire to learn. ... More learning needs to be done at home, in offices and kitchens, in the contexts where knowledge is deployed to solve problems and add value to people's lives. (Leadbeater, 2000, pp. 111–112)

Literature

(Concern about) corrupting effects of television, advertising, and the mass media
in general ... (reflects) teachers' and administrators' inability to recognize that we
are no longer living in a purely literary culture, that the current generation will get
a large proportion of its information and values from films, television, and radio.
(Silberman, 1970, p. 186)

In *Classroom Cinema*, Maynard (1977) found that far and away the
most frequent users of film in the classroom were English teachers.
Moreover, where schools went so far as to hold a film class, it was
generally located in the curriculum of the English department. Robin
Morgan (1998) points out a similar genealogy for cultural studies: it
appears most frequently in the classes of high school English instruc-
tors. Even the discipline as a whole started in an English department,
in Birmingham University, England, and several of its early founding
figures were literary scholars.

This educational lineage may help to explain why film has come
to serve as an adjunct to the literary canon. It is typically seen as a
"postliterary" or "paraliterary" medium, as an alternative narrative
form, thereby downplaying its perceptual quality, its position in visual
culture, and its aesthetic status. The films chosen most for English teaching are movies based on novels, not films chosen for their own cinematic
quality or educational potential (Schreiber, 1947). Peters (1961) has even
suggested that film-teaching, especially the appreciation component, is
so close to literature teaching that it could most reasonably be "housed
along with the latter" (p. 87).

Maynard found two major uses of film in English classes: as moti-
vation to read a piece of literature, or as "reading reinforcement." In
the former case, the film is shown before the students read the novel.
In the latter, the screening of the film comes after the book is read,
as a "treat" or to "clarify the content" (p. 82). "I've most often seen
this approach work well with films of Shakespeare's plays" (ibid.)[4]
As clarifiers, films serve primarily to illustrate, a logical extension
of the use of illustrations in some literary texts, an approach that
relies on "utilizing media in a transparent manner" (Morgan, 1998,
p. 110). Maynard raises a third or "cross media" usage, which involves

"a detailed comparison of the similarities and differences between a printed work of literature and its cinematic counterpart" (ibid.), including consideration of how textual narrative is replaced by visual language. Nonetheless, he admits that his ulterior motive is to reveal "the film medium as a true extension of the language arts curriculum" (p. 85).

Maynard admits, however, that the didactic use of film as auxiliary text, clarifying, illustrating, or extending the literary one, flies in the face of the fact that "great works of literature—stories, novels, poems, plays—almost never translate well on the screen" (Maynard, 1977, p. 83). He cites Anthony Burgess's argument that the most successful translations tend to be from pop literature not the classics.[5]

A similar shortcoming obtains with filmic dramatizations claiming to translate particular historical episodes. The streamlining and romanticizing of such events always runs the risk of "popularizing," and the resulting distortions tend to rely on and promote trivializations and stereotypes. This is the case, for example, with Disney's *Pocahontas* (Pewewardy, 1996–1997; cf. Gay, 2000, pp. 125–126) and even, though less crassly, Terence Malick's *The New World* (2005). The attraction of using such movies in the classroom, then, would seem to be based on something other than the intent to illustrate or confirm historians' textual accounts.

Text

[T]here is, in the accession to technical culture, a camouflaged and clandestine aspiration to "literate" culture. (Baudrillard, 1990, p. 72)

A substantial part of the opposition to popular culture in education as insufficiently literary remains the historical commitment to the canon of printed texts: "Educators, as defenders of print, have a particular and longstanding problem with TV and popular culture more generally" (C. Luke, 1997, p. 19). Baudrillard's remark above suggests that this textual prejudice is incorporated into all of mass media culture at a technical level. Hence, when media enter educational discourse, they tend to be assimilated to reading and writing by talking about "literacies" and by reducing those to techniques or skills. Further doubts about media education follow, since it does not appear at first glance that there is any easy transition from consumption to production in parallel with the desired movement from reading to writing in the domain of textual literacy. Visual literacy then appears to come out as more strictly passive than textual literacy.

Another version of the textuality argument is presented by Ernest Mandel (1986):

> Specialists in the science of communications are increasingly coming to argue that the replacement of written text by images, of transparent linearity by opaque space, almost inevitably leads to more primitive context, acts regressively upon the content of communication itself. ... Mental structures themselves become involved in the change. ... A reversal to non-written language, to what are essentially more primitive forms of communication, must stimulate pre-logical, ahistorical, and indeed antihistorical, more and more primitive forms of thinking as well. (p. 96)

Here, text is defended by default: its merit is that it escapes the fate of the image. Hence the enemy here may be visual culture rather than popular culture, but given the overlap, popular culture must surely be part of Mandel's intended target. A parallel preference is expressed by Adorno (1981–1982/1966) in relation to those images that appear in film:

> Film is faced with the dilemma of finding a procedure which neither lapses into arts-and-crafts nor slips into a more documentary mode. The obvious answer today, as forty years ago, is that of montage which does not interfere with things but rather arranges them in a constellation akin to that of writing. (p. 203)

According to this rare moment of generosity on Adorno's part, the dubious art of film can be redeemed by being made to resemble in its syntax the traditional written text.

As in *Happy Feet*, the guardians of high culture seem to have their work cut out defending the bastion of entrenched tradition from the inroads of mass culture. The implicit standard of comparison by which movies are made to seem to be falling short of real "culture" is predominantly literary. For example, the president of Bard College, Leon Botstein, a noted classical musician, argues:

> Steven Spielberg's dramatization of the Holocaust ... was fine. But it isn't comparable to a historical document and it isn't comparable to the literature of Primo Levi. It simply isn't. (Botstein, 1998, p. 66)

A similar comparison appears in Johnson's (2005) recent analysis:

> I do not believe that most of today's pop culture is made up of masterpieces that will someday be taught alongside Joyce and Chaucer in college survey courses. (p. 11)

Johnson introduces here another common trope in this area: appealing to the "genius"—the individual of world-historical visibility and significance, who casts such a long shadow that popular culture, which supposedly lacks such figures and their "Great Works," is cast into eternal darkness. As Lunenfeld (2001) states, "[W]ithout the claim of genius, art cannot compete with the juggernaut that is popular culture" (p. 2).

In none of these cases is any evidence or criterion proffered or substantiated. Particularly remarkable is President Botstein's assumption that his opinion is *self-evidently* true—so privileged and unquestionable is this view that he feels it neither deserves nor requires any justification: "it simply is." From within high culture (and in this case, from within higher education) the supremacy of literature over media, of textual over visual, appears absolute, the gap between high and low simply unbridgeable. The historiographic conceit of the "Great Man" makes the chasm yawn even wider.

As we can see from the above examples, in the discourse defending the entrenched tradition of textuality, educators implicitly and often inadvertently align themselves with a position of dominance in the gender hierarchy associated with that tradition: "Central to ... male textual rule is the near seamless historical repression of a female authorial voice" including "the masculinist (mis)representation of the feminine as 'other'" (C. Luke, 1997, p. 21). As the cultural historian Huyssen (1984) has pointed out, under modernism, mass culture has been aligned with the feminine, and so shares in its phenomenal "otherness."

The appeal to text, then, and the aversion to image, to film, or to visual culture in general, tend to link arms with parallel forms of social domination. In *Happy Feet*, it is no surprise, then, that the toe-tapping, stutter-stepping hero, "Mumble," who departs so readily and so far from the traditionally inscribed precepts of the (all male) elders, and makes a "spectacle" of himself, is presented as a distinctly unmasculine, fluffy little fellow, who does not fit easily into the sexist and heterosexist penguin community.

Mass Culture and the Arts

There is a double standard at work with regard to the arts. Insofar as they represent high culture (the opera, the symphony, the museum), they are the polar opposite of mass culture, but insofar as they are subordinated to the sciences, they exist in the same utilitarian limbo as media and popular culture:

> The arts are often made to be intentionally impractical. The number of people who agree that the arts are in some way useful are indeed few. Microsoft wasn't built on arts education, and it is not clear that the future of employment is contingent on the arts. (Botstein, 1998, p. 65)

So much so that enormous efforts are made in education to show that art education involves the acquisition of useful information and teaches "skills," or that it serves to foster advances in other academic subjects— the "handmaiden" role.

However, there is a deeper suspicion of the arts, regarding the threat that their supposed sensuousness may pose to established morality:

> In this country there is an enormous fear of the arts, … because they seem to have some competitive role with religion. … The arts are considered in some way critical of moral standards; they are iconoclastic, and, regardless of content, they compete for the souls of the public. … The notion that there is something inherently seductive in artistic expression, in the sense of the opposition between sexuality and morality, creates a suspicion of the arts as related in part

to unbridled sensuality. … I think that one cannot help but confront the residual and diverse religious reactions to the arts in relationship to the question of how these might function in education. The "competition," those invested in religion, fear the artist-as-charismatic-figure. (Botstein, 1998, pp. 64–65)

As if to confirm his own theory, Botstein then goes on to characterize the scope of popular culture as "Madonna, MTV, dramatizations on film of gore, destruction, violence, beheading, dismemberment and rape" (p. 65). Pop culture, confounded here with visual media, appears, then, to condense and exaggerate the immorality of the arts in the most flagrant of ways—captured best in the depraved combination of sex and violence.

Rather than seeing sexuality and aggressivity as important aspects of human nature with significant implications for both sociality and schooling, educators tend to denigrate them—for example, media educator, Ross (2004–2005) reduces them to "thrills and chills" taken advantage of by opportunistic "sideshow hustlers who market the sordid" (p. 658). He sounds the alarm for "the damage done by having these type people and their messages pumped, unchallenged, into our children's minds," such that "(n)ow we are truly in a desperate situation" (ibid.). Such warnings echo earlier concerns, as, for instance, this voice from the president of the influential Association for Educational Communications and Technology, who sees the hustling and the pumping as a mandate for teacher intervention:

> [T]he possibilities for the corruption of taste and morals which constitute the sole alternative to sound educational approach in this field impose this inescapable task upon the school. (Hochheimer, 1939, p. 7)

Commercialism

> Despite its virtue, a feature film is necessarily part of a money-making entertainment agenda. In a sense, that is the overwhelming agenda. It's a kind of very successful entertainment. But there's usually something more to art. (Botstein, 1998, p. 66)

Another primary concern is *commercialism,* as though youth are particularly susceptible to materialistic values and should be prevented as long as possible from becoming consumers. This criticism of popular culture has come not only from the right but also from the left, as for example in Hoggart (2004) and particularly in Adorno and Horkheimer (1972/1945):

> Movies and radio no longer pretend to be art. The truth that they are just business is made into an ideology in order to justify the rubbish they deliberately produce. They call themselves industries. ... Automobiles, bombs, and movies keep the whole thing together until their leveling element shows its strength in the very wrong that is furthered. (Adorno & Horkheimer, 1993/1945, p. 31)

There is an implicit assumption in the Frankfurt School of thought, fostered more recently by Barber (2001), that consumption is a purely privatized activity, and hence in opposition to the public presence, judgment, and voice that citizenship require. Presumably engagement in production escapes this critique, although one could argue along with the *1844 Manuscripts* that it is in the productive process that alienation arises, or with the *Grundrisse* that production and consumption are not easily separable in the first place.

Certainly, there is reason for skepticism about the way teenagers have been "branded" by and for the marketplace (Quart, 2003), tempted away from subversive and insubordinate activities by the seductive appeal of teen culture commodities (Savage, 2007). However, research evidence would suggest that it is precisely in spontaneous consumerism, or more accurately "post-consumption" activities, that contemporary youth acquire individuality, spontaneity, sociality, the cultivation of sophisticated taste, and the development of a grounded aesthetic of life (Willis, 1990; cf. Skelton & Valentine, 1997).

Moreover, there is a certain hypocrisy in educators claiming the moral high ground for schools as nonmaterialistic enclaves of anticonsumerism that protect youth from corruption by the economic world. The fact is that the conditions under which young people learn are very much dictated by debates over funding; in New York State this has become a major legal issue of late.

At the federal level, smokescreens like "No Child Left Behind" (NCLB)—an unfortunate military metaphor, if ever there was one— only thinly disguise a number of ulterior motives. Behind the NCLB priorities of disaggregated test scores and psychometric accountability lie the agendas of privatization and marketization. We are witnessing a pervasive shift toward a conservative "audit culture," regulated by managerial discourse. This audit culture is centered on the anti-democratic use of corporate criteria to measure and assess employee effectiveness, a punitive regime inspiring widespread evaluation anxiety driven by the underlying threat that private firms will be recruited to take over "failing" institutions (Apple, 2006).

As Apple points out, within this game plan, even apparently democratic initiatives have been co-opted. Home schooling, for example, is being absorbed into the fiscally opportunistic "home school charter" movement. The controlling policy of the current Republican administration is to restrict public expenditures on education by any means possible, especially in a time when the military budget for belligerent overseas occupations is so vigorously sapping our resources.

The capitalization of students in education is not restricted to external influences. Secondary schooling (not to mention higher education) still has a strong vocational message as lampooned so effectively in the recent pop movie, *Accepted* (2006). If anything, secondary schooling is regulated by a strictly "human capital" worldview, which measures knowledge and skills in practical and technical terms as a function of the social capital that they underwrite (Willis, 1977). The very term "excellence," so widely used as an all-purpose criterion of achievement in schools and graduate schools of education, is itself passed down from the corporate world (Lewis, 1986; cf. Molnar, 1996).

The current emphasis on standards and achievement, the increasing stress on educational credentials and pre-professional qualifications, and the turning of the home into a surrogate workplace

> are driven by—or at least inextricably connected with—the work of commercial corporations. ... (Schools) have reorganized themselves on commercial principles. ... Most obviously, we are now seeing a gradual privatization of schooling. ... [C]ompanies with interests in very different areas, such as super-markets, are increasingly keen to promote themselves as sponsors of education. ... These initiatives reflect the general ascendancy of "promotional culture." ... [R]esources from the private sphere ... are increasingly being used to supplement shortfalls in public provision. (Buckingham & Scanlon, 2003, pp. 3–5)

Ironically, this privatizing sponsorship and promotion is rampant in high culture as well, such that the institutionalized arts—museums, opera companies, orchestras, and various societies—are more dependent on corporate support and control than ever before (Gans, 1999). Museum gift shops are an example of how far institutions of high art are willing to go in the direction of commodifying and marketing themselves. The traditional alignment of school curricula with high culture could therefore be said to be undergoing consolidation by a shared process of professionalization/privatization/corporatization that is radically transforming both in the same direction, synthesizing them in accordance with a common commercial objective.

Adulthood

The preoccupation of moral panickers with kids' exposure to sex and violence disguises the important observation that these are two major domains in the traditional territory of adults. This is a clue to a further reason for the opposition to popular culture in education: the fear of young people being tainted too early with adulthood. The adjective "adult" in "adult movies," for example, already indicates how pejoratively we think of our own human maturity. Even "adult swim" now connotes, not pool policy but a Cartoon Network program and Internet Web site featuring all manner of risqué, late-night fare.

Just because there is moral panic about exposure to sex and violence does not mean that sexuality and aggression are not frequently represented in the media. One might go so far as to venture that the life of love and hate—of reproduction and death, or more generally of impulse and satisfaction—is precisely the domain that the media deal with best. If there remains any validity to Freud's claim that Eros and Thanatos together rule the unconscious then, along with Bataille (1986), Marcuse (1957) and Leslie Fiedler (1960), we should not be shocked that these two principles—and moreover the dialectic between them—are found to regulate our cultural unconscious. There is little that is surprising about *General Hospital, St. Elsewhere, E.R., Grey's Anatomy, Scrubs, Nurse Betty, A Hospital Romance, Carry on Doctor, Doctor in the House,* and so on. Given the association of emotional life and the body with "low" functions, we should perhaps expect that (outside of opera) the carnal and the cadaverous appear most frequently and vividly in popular culture.

Because we confuse popular culture with youth culture (especially by lumping them together as the "mass media") and since youth, too, rank "low" on the social scale, it makes sense that parents and educators alike are concerned that popular culture is exposing adolescents to adult issues (Postman, 1994/1982). Such domains as love and aggression remain highly charged and conflicted for adults, even though their authority depends on posing as mature "grown ups." Concealing this embarrassing paradox requires a certain defensiveness, which emerges as excessive protectionism toward "children," with a hypertrophied pop psychology rhetoric of "youthful innocence" and "growing up too fast." This despite the fact that the research of Lesko (2001), Buckingham (2003), and others indicates that it is keeping youth "socially young" that occasions the most damaging developmental problems.

In the area of visual culture, there has been nothing more heavily policed than the boundary between family and adult entertainment. The caesura between "G" and "PG" was initially the focus of attention, but these days the critical distinction seems to be between "PG13" and "R" (Teasley & Wilder, 1997). *Little Miss Sunshine* has been a controversial recent case in point: a light comedy about a family road trip, with a young child star, and a G-rated title, yet officially rated "R" because of granddad's occasional swear words.

The line is obscured by the fact that many "adult" feature films deal with obviously juvenile issues, especially in the matters of sex and aggression, and commercial movies are often directed to both adult and teen markets, for patent fiscal reasons. Media educators such as Ross (2004–2005) admit that "adolescent culture needs to be in opposition to adult culture" yet, as Peters' (1961) early studies indicate and recent updates confirm (e.g., Shary, 2005; Matika, 2008), movies are a primary way in which the adult world is made less incomprehensible and less frightening to youth so that the transition from adolescence to adulthood may eventually be facilitated.

Peters points out also that, developmentally speaking, by high school age virtually all the mature cinematic viewing capacities required of adults are already in place. In light of this, then, the problem for the conservative agenda of controlling adolescent access to adult media is that, regardless of the absence of cinematic education in schools and the lack of preparation in educators to teach it, young people appear to be developing prodigious abilities to grasp mature visual culture. Arguably, this is because the world of film and allied media is one of the few resources available for youth to learn about crucial issues in social development—and for reasons that are not entirely apparent, one of the least censored.

Conclusion

School makes alienation preparatory to life, thus depriving education of reality and work of creativity. School prepares for the alienating institutionalization of life by teaching the need to be taught. Once this lesson is learned, people lose their incentive to grow in independence. (Illich, 2002/1970, p. 47)

According to Illich's analysis, which in turn resembles the earlier critique by Jules Henry (1963), schools tend to conventionalize learning, making it dependent on teaching and hence less creative. Normative schooling is a kind of nontransferable meta-learning that works to restrict the capacity to learn how to learn in new ways.

As the earlier quotation from Buckingham and Scanlon points out above, a major part of the problem is "what we count as learning in the first place." Clearly, from their empirical work, we can see how schools tend to discount certain types of learning for contingent reasons. They tend to dismiss the unconventional kinds (e.g., learning without a teacher, learning from games, learning from performance) not because they are not backed by educational theory or research but because they are the kinds of learning that tend to occur outside school, informally, and in the absence of any specific, identifiable methodology. One suspects that the rationale behind such exclusionary practices has something to do with professionalism, and dilemmas in this regard are likely linked to the current crisis in education.

A further reason for the conservatism of even liberal teachers in this regard may have to do with the substantial "perspective transformation" (Mezirow, 1978) that may be required in order to arrive at a broader approach to admissible learnings. As Mezirow, Sullivan (2005; Sullivan, Morrell, & O'Connor, 2002), and others have shown, it is not just a technical question of acquiring new skills, acquiring new knowledge, or recalibrating one's practices. Rather, such perspective upgrading requires an extensive personal transformation, one that can be quite challenging, exhaustive, and extended in time.

A notable case in point is Gee's (2003) account of his own conversion experience, which (perhaps not coincidentally) took place in the home. He was first struck with the degree of intensity and involvement of video game play in his own son: "I thought ... Wouldn't it be great if kids were willing to put in this much time on task on such challenging material in school and enjoy it so much?" (p. 5). When he tried to play a video game for the first time himself (one based on H. G.Wells), he was surprised:

> It was for me profoundly difficult. This game—and this turned out to be true of video games more generally—requires the player to learn and think in ways in which I am not adept. Suddenly, all my baby-boomer ways of learning and thinking, for which I had heretofore received ample rewards, did not work. ... I found playing *Time Machine* a "life-enhancing experience." (ibid.)

Video games shift the terms of pedagogy by subverting established notions of learning, and hence altering our criteria for what schooling should include:

> It is not surprising that many politicians, policy-makers, and their academic fellow travelers who think poor children should be content with schooling for service jobs don't like video games. They say they don't like them because they are violent. But, in reality, video games do violence to these people's notions of what makes learning powerful and schools good and fair. (ibid.)

Gee went on to conduct a rather complex and thorough study of video games, the central conclusion of which was

> [V]ideo games ... operate with—that is, they build into their designs and encourage—good principles of learning, principles that are better than those in many of our skill-and-drill, back-to-basics, test-them-until-they-drop schools. (p. 205)

It was the monkey psychologist Harry Harlow who long ago defined intelligence as the ability to learn about learning, and human (or animal) development as a process of learning how to learn. It may be that what Gee found in both his own adult confrontation with video games and his study of kids playing them is the meta-lesson that they are equipped to convey: the relearning of how to learn.

This chance may well be a tacit contributor to the enormous appeal of such games. It may also be a reason for the enormous resistance to them within established institutions, because they do violence to customary assumptions about how learning can, does, and should take place. While those engaged in the business of maintaining the educational system may not change their minds about popular culture, popular culture is already in the business of changing minds.

Notes

1. I would like to thank Matt Carlin, Jim Feast, Julian Henriques and Alissa Quart for urging me to break the spell of obsessive parenting to spill some ink again. Randall Allsup, John Baldacchino, and Elisabeth Johnson contributed lively conversations and stimulating correspondence. Ryan Goble and Maria Hamilton provided valuable bibliographic information and Bora Kim and Tanzina Taher gave invaluable clerical support. Ingrid, Eleanor and Farallon generously allowed me time and space, at some inconvenience to their own feet, for which enduring gratitude is due.

2. On the relation of power to visual space (in addition to the work of Foucault's middle period), see Lefebvre (1991). I have attempted to illuminate the politics of verticality elsewhere, in the context of violence (Broughton, 1995, 1996) and the institutions of development and education (Broughton, 1987).

3. The opposition between formal education and fast food is illustrated in *Fast Times at Ridgmont High* when Spicoli (Sean Penn's stoner character) uses a surreptitious pizza order to interrupt the class being conducted by Mr. Hand.

4. Not only is it the case that "Shakespeare has become the symbolic talisman of cultural value" but also "The purpose of reading Shakespeare, according to this perspective, is not just a matter of learning to appreciate what is self-evidently good: it is also about learning to see through what is self-evidently *bad*" (Buckingham & Sefton-Green, 1994, p. 2). In other words, the Shakespearian criterion, marking the apex of Eurocentrism, serves at one and the same time to define the sacred quality of high- and school culture, and to exclude profane low

culture. One could be forgiven for wondering if such constant recourse to Shakespeare, and Shakespeare alone, means that critics of popular culture simply can't remember the names of any other playwrights, let alone any dramatic writing outside the English language. That, in turn, would seem to be evidence that the "classical" education they received, and which they recall with nostalgia, somehow managed to produce in its students not only a cultural xenophobia but also a systematic ignorance about their own high culture. Of course, Shakespearian drama was originally part of low culture (Levine, 1990), as confirmed by the location of The Globe theater amid the homeless encampments of the South Bank.

5.   Christopher Durang (1997/1978) argues lyrically, in *A History of the American Film*, that our formative emotional learning is modeled on scenes and characters from mainstream movies.

References

Adorno, Theodor & Max Horkheimer (1972/1945). The Culture Industry. In *Dialectic of Enlightenment* (pp. 121–161). New York: Seabury.

Adorno, Theodor (1981–1982). Transparencies on film. *New German Critique*, 24–25, 198–216.

Apple, Michael (2006). Who "No Child Left Behind" Leaves Behind. In *Educating the "Right" Way: Markets, Standards, God, and Inequality* (pp. 87–123). New York: Routledge.

Bataille, Georges (1985). *Visions of Excess*. Minneapolis: University of Minnesota Press.

Bataille, Georges (1986). *Death and Sensuality*. San Francisco: City Lights.

Baudrillard, Jean (1990). Mass Media Culture. In *Revenge of the Crystal* (pp. 63–97). London, UK: Pluto.

Benjamin, Walter (1969). The Work of Art in the Age of Reproduction. In *Illuminations*. New York: Schocken. http://bid.berkeley.edu/bidclass/readings/benjamin.html

Botstein, Leon (1998). What Role for the Arts? In William Ayers & Janet Miller (Eds.), *A Light in Dark Times: Maxine Greene and the Unfinished Conversation* (pp. 62–70). New York: Teachers College Press.

Broughton, John (1987). The Masculine Authority of the Cognitive. In Barbel Inhelder & Denis de Caprona (Eds.), *Piaget Today*. Hillsdale. NJ: Lawrence Erlbaum.

Broughton, John (1995). The Bomb in the Bathroom: Anality in High-Tech Warfre. In Ian Lubek, Gail Pheterson & Charles Toman (Eds.), *Recent Issues in Theoretical Psychology. Vol. 4*. New York: Springer.

Broughton, John (1996). U.S. Over Iraq: Hi-Tech Weaponry and Low Culture in the Gulf War. In Charles Strozier & Michael Flynn (Eds.), *Genocide, War, and Human Survival: Festschrift for Robert Lifton* (pp. 106–123). New York: Rowman & Littlefield.

Bruner, Jerome (1987). *Actual Minds, Possible Worlds*. Cambridge, MA: Harvard University Press.

Bruner, Jerome (1991). The narrative construction of reality. *Critical Inquiry*, 18(1), 1–21.

Buckingham, David (2003). *Media Education: Literacy, Learning, and Contemporary Culture*. Cambridge, UK: Polity Press.

Buckingham, David & Margaret Scanlon (2003). Going Interactive: The Pedagogy of Edutainment Software. In *Education, Entertainment and Learning in the Home* (pp. 109–125). Milton Keynes, UK: Open University Press.

Buckingham, David & Sefton-Green, Julian (1994). *Cultural Studies Goes to School*. London: UK: Taylor & Francis.

Collodi, Carlo (1968/1880). *The Adventures of Pinocchio*. New York: Lancer Books.

Dolby, Nadine (2003). Popular culture and democratic practice. *Harvard Educational Review*, 73, 258–284.

Durang Christopher (1997/1978). *A History of the American Film*. New York: Avon Books.

Fear, David (2005). The big picture. *Time Out New York*, Jan. 6–12, 85.

Fiedler, Leslie (1960). *Love and Death in the American Novel*. New York: Criterion Books.

Gans, Herbert (1999). *Popular Culture and High Culture*, 2nd ed. New York: Basic Books.

Gay, Geneva (2000). *Culturally Responsive Teaching*. New York: Teachers College Press.

Gee, James Paul (2003). *What Video Games Have to Teach Us about Learning and Literacy*. New York: Palgrave.

Gitlin, Tod (1996). Some Reflections on 20th Century Violence and the Soft Apocalypse. In Charles Strozier & Michael Flynn (Eds.), *Trauma and Self* (pp. 59–68). New York: Rowman & Littlefield.

Gould, Stephen Jay (1993). Dinomania. *New York Review of Books*, 40(14), 17–20.

Hall, Stuart & Paddy Whannel (1964). *The Popular Arts: A Critical Guide to the Mass Media*. Boston: Beacon Press.

Henry, Jules (1963). *Culture against Man*. New York: Random House.

Hochheimer, Rita (1939). *Motion Picture Discrimination in Schools*. Wilmette, IL: Encyclopedia Britannica Films.

Hoggart, Richard (2004). *Mass Media in a Mass Society: Myth and Reality*. London: Continuum International Publishing Group.

Huyssen, Andreas (1984). Mass Culture as Woman: Modernism's Other. *After the Great Divide*. Bloomington: Indiana University Press.

Illich, Ivan (2002/1970). *Deschooling Society*. New York: Marion Boyars.

Johnson, Steven (2005). *Everything Bad for You Is Good*. New York: Riverhead Press.

Kanter, Rosabeth Moss (1972). The organization child: Experience management in a nursery school. *Sociology of Education*, 45(2), 186–211.

Kovel, Joel (1978). Rationalization and the family. *Telos*, 37, 5–21.

Kundera, Milan (2007). Die Weltliteratur: How we read one another. *New Yorker*, Jan. 8, 28–35.

Leadbeater, C. (2000). *Living on Thin Air: The New Economy*. London: Penguin.

Lefebvre, Henri (1991). *The Production of Space.* New York: Blackwell.

Lesko, Nancy (2001). *Act Your Age: A Cultural Construction of Adolescence.* New York: Routledge.

Levine, Lawrence (1990). *Highbrow/Lowbrow: The Emergence of Cultural Hierarchy in America.* Reprint ed. Cambridge, MA: Harvard.

Lewis, James (1986). *Creating Excellence in our Schools: By Taking More Lessons from America's Best-Run Companies.* Westbury, NY: J. L. Wilkerson Publishing Co.

Lifton, Robert (1967). *Death in Life.* New York: Random House.

Luke, Carmen (1997). Media Literacy and Cultural Studies. In Sandy Musspratt, Allan Luke, & Peter Freebody (Eds.), *Constructing Critical Literacies: Teaching and Learning Textual Practice* (pp. 19–49). Cresskill, NJ: Hampton Press.

Lunenfeld, Peter (2001). *Snap to Grid: A User's Guide to Digital Arts, Media and Cultures.* Cambridge, MA: MIT Press.

Mandel, Ernest (1986). *Delightful Murder.* Minneapolis, MN: University of Minnesota Press.

March, Tom (2005–2006). The New WWW: Whatever, Whenever, Wherever. *Educational Leadership,* Dec.–Jan., 14–19.

Marcuse, Herbert (1957). *Eros and Civilization.* Boston, MA: Beacon Press.

Marcuse, Herbert (1978). *The Aesthetic Dimension.* Boston, MA: Beacon Press.

Matika, Alison (2008). *Responses of High School Boys and Girls to Cinematic Violence: Implications for Secondary School English Teachers.* Unpublished doctoral dissertation, Teachers College, Columbia University.

Maynard, Richard (1977). *Classroom Cinema.* New York: Teachers College Press.

Mezirow, Jack (1978). *Education for Perspective Transformation.* New York: Center for Adult Education, Teachers College, Columbia University.

Mirzoeff, Nicholas (1999). *An Introduction to Visual Culture.* New York: Routledge.

Molnar, Alex (1996). *Giving Kids the Business: The Commercialization of America's Schools.* Boulder, CO: Westview.

Morgan, Robert (1998). Provocations for a Media Education in Small Letters. In David Buckingham (Ed.), *Teaching Popular Culture* (pp. 107–131). London, UK: University College of London Press.

Pellegrini, Anthony (Ed.) (1995). *The Future of Play Theory: Multidisciplinary Inquiry into the Contributions of Brian Sutton-Smith.* Albany, NY: State University of New York Press.

Peters, J. M. L. (1961). *Teaching about Film.* New York: Columbia University Press International Documents Service.

Pewewardy, C. (1996–1997). The Pocahontas Paradox: A cautionary tale for Educators. *Journal of Navaho Education,* 14(1–2), 20–25.

Postman, Neil (1986). *Amusing Ourselves to Death: Public Discourse in the Age of Show Business.* New York: Penguin.

Postman, Neil (1994/1982). *The Disappearance of Childhood.* New York: Vintage.

Price, David A. (2005). *Love and Hate in Jamestown: John Smith, Pocahontas, and the Heart of New Nation.* New York: Vintage.

Quart, Alissa (2003). *Branded: The Buying and Selling of Teenagers.* New York: Perseus.

Ross, Terrence (2004–2005). Media empowerment via the best and worst: A dialectic approach to teaching media literacy to our children. *International Journal of Learning,* 11, 657–662.

Savage, Jon (2007). *Teenage: The Creation of Youth Culture.* New York: Viking (U.S.).

Schreiber, Robert (1947). Literary works for the educational screen. *The English Journal,* 36(1), 29–34.

Sealey, Kelvin Shawn (2006). *Spectacle as a site of critical pedagogy: A multiple case study of college audiences' responses to performative entertainment-education events.* Unpublished doctoral dissertation, Teachers College, Columbia University.

Shary, Timothy (2005). *Teen Movies: American Youth on Screen.* New York: Wallflower.

Silberman, Charles (1970). *Crisis in the Classroom.* New York: Random House.

Singhal, Arvind & Everett Rogers (1999). *Entertainment-Education: A Communication Strategy for Social Change.* Hillsdale, NJ: Lawrence Erlbaum.

Singhal, Arvind, Michael Cody, Everett Rogers, & Miguel Sabido (Eds.) (2003). *Entertainment-Education and Social Change: History, Research and Practice.* Hillsdale, NJ: Lawrence Erlbaum.

Skelton, Tracy & Gill Valentine (Eds.) (1997). *Cool Places: Geographies of Youth Cultures.* New York: Routledge.

Sobol, Thomas (2006). Farewell for Sobol and Reid. *Inside Teachers College,* 11(7), 11.

Storey, John (2003). *Inventing the Popular.* Malden, MA: Blackwell.

Storey, John (2006). *Cultural Theory and Popular Culture,* 2nd edn. Harlow, UK: Pearson Education.

Strinati, Dominic (2004). *An Introduction to Theories of Popular Culture.* New York: Routledge.

Sullivan, Edmund (2005). *Transformative Learning: Educational Vision for the 21st Century.* London: Zed Books.

Sullivan, Edmund, Amish Morrell, & Mary Ann O'Connor (2002). *Expanding the Boundaries of Transformative Learning: Essays on Theory and Praxis.* New York: Palgrave.

Sutton-Smith, Brian (1980). *Play and Learning.* New York: Wiley.

Sutton-Smith, Brian (2001/1997). *The Ambiguity of Play.* Cambridge, MA: Harvard University Press.

Tavin, Kevin (2000). Just Doing It: Towards a Critical Thinking of Visual Culture. In Danny Weil & Holly Kathleen Anderson (Eds.), *Perspectives in Critical Thinking: Essays by Teachers in Theory and Practice,* pp. 187–210. New York: Peter Lang.

Teasley, Alan & Wilder, Ann (1996). *Reel Conversations: Reading Films with Young Adults.* Portsmouth, NH: Boynton/Cook.

Willis, Paul (1981/1977). *Learning to Labor.* New York: Columbia University Press.

Willis, Paul (1990). *Common Culture.* Boulder, CO: Westview Press.

Winn, Marie (1977). *The Plug-in Drug: Television, Children and the Family.* New York: Penguin.

Winnicott, Donald (1970). *Playing and Reality.* London, UK: Penguin.

Chapter Two

Popular Culture
and the Politics
of Revolutionary Education

ANNETTE LOUISE BICKFORD

Consider, to begin with, interpretations from both high and low culture of a colonial scene: the "discovery" of America as an eroticized encounter. Writing about the European conquest of America in 1492, Samuel Eliot Morison mused,

> *Never again may mortal men hope to recapture the amazement, the wonder, the delight of those October days in 1492 when the New World gracefully yielded her virginity to the conquering Castilians* (Shohat and Stam, 1994:141).

Similarly, Sir Walter Raleigh described *"...a country that hath yet her mayden head, never sakt, turned nor wrought"* (Montrose, 1991:12). Colonial discourses have historically operated through eroticized tropes of virgin land, whereby the feminization of the New World permitted the allegorical interpretation of invasion and conquest to be a matter of natural gender hierarchy (McClintock, 1995: 24-30). Explorers' protocolonialist interpretations of discovery suggest allegorical personifications of the New World as empty virgin land, uncultivated, undomesticated, and without legitimate owners (Spurr, 1993; Shohat and Stam, 1994:141;

McClintock, 1995:30). Jan van der Straet's widely disseminated drawing (ca. 1575) of explorer Amerigo Vespucci's encounter with America portrays "primitive" nations as the epitome of sexual excess and aberration, the aboriginal Other as naked and sexually submissive. Historical discourses of European geopolitical conquest employ mutually exclusive binaries of sexual excess vs. the rationally ordered Western subject; instinctual, feminized savagery vs. masculine knowledge and civilization:

> Vespucci, the godlike arrival, is destined to inseminate her with the male seeds of civilisation, fructify the wilderness and quell the riotous scenes of cannibalism in the background. America allegorically represents nature's invitation to conquest, while Vespucci, gripping the fetish instruments of imperial mastery–astrolabe, flag and sword–confronts the virgin land with the patrimony of scientific mastery and imperial might (McClintock, 1995: 26).

Popular culture conveys the same messages in a new form. Disney's film production *Pocahontas* establishes Pocahontas' significatory role as *terra incognita*, a feminine boundary marker of imperialism (McClintock, 1995:24), steeping Western imperialism in high romance. This popular film relies on colonial tropes of animalization, eroticization and infantilization, as well as rape/rescue fantasies, where Pocahontas's grandmother is a tree, and her best friend, a raccoon. Signifying virgin land, Pocahontas is erotically inviting and confounded by John Smith's "spinning arrow," his compass; a "fetish instrument" of imperial mastery. Disney's Other is reminiscent of the protocolonialist Other, as well as current constructions of "visible minorities" and the Other in ostensibly developing countries.[1]

These interpretations of "discovery," whether expressed through high or low culture, demonstrate that different forms do not guarantee varying content. The Disney Corporation affords wide access to an explanation of imperial conquest that is very much in keeping with the more sophisticated accounts of Jan van der Straet and Sir Walter Raleigh. Colonial tropes and perceptions of politically immature, "savage" peoples without history continue to register as common sense; seemingly harmless when disseminated as light-hearted diversion. It does not necessarily follow, as many advocates of the use of popular culture in education imagine, that such texts are essentially and axiomatically emancipatory in their effect, in keeping with the subject positions and presumed structural interests of those who generate them.

In the interest of accessible learning, popular culture is being incorporated into education, increasingly legitimized as a pedagogical method that extends participation in education to those who, for various reasons, do not respond to esoteric texts or the written word. Celebrating popular culture as an emancipatory pedagogical tool, and committed to social transformation through action as opposed to mere words, informal educators often work within a binary model of theory vs. practice, prioritizing practice over theory, overlooking or even rejecting the importance of content analysis. The work of Nadine Dolby, for instance, illustrates this celebratory approach to informal pedagogy within formal education. Dolby anticipates that as low culture, popular culture axiomatically if gradually, through the co-opting of small spaces resistant to neoliberalism, produces social justice through democratic practice. For Dolby (2003: 258), popular culture "should be understood as a cultural practice that has its own power to create social change—to alter social conditions and the very foundation of people's lives."

It behooves us to offer alternative ways of learning to foster accessible education; but it is equally important to be mindful about the kinds of messages we communicate. Adding popular culture texts to curricula is no panacea. While talk can be useless, promoting action uninformed by theoretical reflexivity runs the risk of reifying what we mean to change, as the Pocahontas/Vespucci example demonstrates.

High culture and pop cultural forms are mere conduits, easily bearing the same content. Limitless access to films like Disney's *Pocahontas* confers little inclusivity upon the multitude,[2] inadvertently exacerbating oppressive relations through the wide dissemination of confining stereotypes, rooted in problematic historical interpretations. Accessibility is not enough, and then, it can be too much. Informal educators propose that popular culture in education fosters democratic practice, whereby everyone has a voice (Dolby, 2003: 258–260), but dominant discourses are still decidedly hierarchical despite the huge expansion in participation that the mainstream engenders, subsequently precluding truly inclusive democratic participation. In other words, popular culture in education may afford equal opportunity to participate through wider accessibility, but on uneven ground where participation cannot be exercised wholly and in equivalent ways, inclusivity is limited, and efforts to participate on others' terms deepen oppressive practices because it seems as though everyone has a voice, if only they would use it.

Popular culture is enormously complex, generating limitless and unpredictable exchanges, and is indispensable in education, I will argue, when it is used in conjunction with critical theory. While popular culture can disseminate detrimental messages far and wide, it can also be, as *informed practice*, a vehicle for widely inclusive participation and revolutionary social transformation; but it is up to us to make it so.

We can maneuver the use of popular culture in education into informed practice through critical thinking. As thought assessing other thought, critical methodology aids in the deconstruction of naturalized assumptions and helps us transcend constraining normalizing discourses. In addition, it facilitates Weberian *verstehen* through dialogue that strives for intellectual empathy and emotional connectedness, eroding the barriers of social hierarchies that breed racism, heteronormativity, sexism and other hierarchical relationships that impede solidarity. As part of intellectual empathy, *verstehen* inspires a passionate will for social transformation, effected through dynamic and dialogic collaborations of various interest groups. We could more effectively improve social conditions with bolder educational initiatives that meld action and critical thinking. It would require our active but observant embracing of popular culture in education until the participatory action afforded by popular culture and the mindfulness fostered by critical thinking (action and reflexivity) are coincident; until education employs popular culture *along* with esoteric texts to explain things but more importantly, that we, as heterogeneous groups of participants in popular culture, may use education as a commonly run (non-state) institutional site for self-directed empathic and creative collaboration that would also involve learning through practice. Education needs revolutionary transformation and revolutionary transformation needs access to critical pedagogy.

Adding popular culture to education constitutes political action encouraging popular participation. Subsequent learning would come through that practice, and would resolve difficult binaries between theory and action; but as I will argue in this chapter, egalitarian political practice could be further deepened if it is informed not just experientially, but also through self-directed, empathic critical reflexivity. Critical-thinking skills enable social transformation through active learning of creative dialogue that avoids the imposition of ideas on others. Because critical thinking skills are a vehicle and not an imposed set of values, the practice would complement the kinds of learning that come from practices of self-rule, actually pre-empting the need for binaries of high and low culture, top-down and bottom-up social transitions, theory and practice. While instrumental as a tool that hones our ability to think independently, critical methodology also calls on us to act on this knowledge we secure for ourselves.

Libertarian Pluralism in Popular Pedagogy

Objections to the incorporation of popular culture as pedagogical methodology are raised by detractors from the Right and Left: conservatives like Matthew Arnold, E. D. Hirsch and William Bennett oppose popular culture for its dilution of high culture, and Frankfurt School anti-populists such as Max Horkheimer and Theodor Adorno reject it not for dumbing down high culture, but as a stupefying conduit in its own right that manipulatively thwarts independent thinking, perpetuating class oppression (Dolby, 2003: 261). Pierre Bourdieu reminds us that distinctions made between high and low culture through cultural signifiers such as taste function primarily to perpetuate class distinctions and the work of such German critical theorists as Walter Benjamin make clear the potential for political resistance within popular culture milieus.

In her article, "Popular Culture and Democratic Practice," (*Harvard Educational Review*, 2003), Nadine Dolby nicely brings together informal and formal education, arguing for the inclusion of popular culture texts in the curriculum as a way of inviting marginalized groups of students to participate more meaningfully in their own education. Dolby

(2003: 258–260) more problematically seeks to demonstrate that despite being "largely driven by commercial interests, which are private and concerned with profit," and notwithstanding a disquietingly pervasive presence of racism, heterosexism, and other oppressive forms within it, popular culture "is a site where people have a voice, a stake, and an interest," through the co-opting of small discursive spaces, a pedagogical experience fostering inclusive democratic practice. Eschewing what might be called armchair politics, Dolby gives considerable attention to uninformed practice. Michael Hardt (2007: xx) resolves the difficult binary between learning and practice to a good extent in his examination of the revolutionary writings of Thomas Jefferson, suggesting participatory democracy as a vehicle for change; for self-training imbricated in the process of actually practicing self-rule; but that instrumental learning would still benefit from critical theory. Hardt (2007: xviii–xx) notes that while recognizing the importance of schools and libraries as essential for the creation of new "knowledges that can sustain democratic self-government," Jefferson's central concern was his proposal of autonomous wards or "little republics" of active self-rule at the local level. Hardt (2007: xix) observes that, "Creating a new human nature, for Jefferson as for Lenin, is a matter of training and habits." Moreover, "people are transformed by practicing autonomy and participating in government … people only learn democracy by doing it" (Hardt, 2007: xx). Dolby's argument for actively changing curricula by bringing popular culture into education runs parallel to this to the extent that she calls for the active engagement in the extension of widespread participation, from which practice will come democratic practice, altering social conditions to reflect a more "just and equitable society" (Dolby, 2003: 258–259, 263).

I am in favor of informed action that is cyclically informed both through periodic reassessment (Hardt, 2007) and circularly, as suggested by the metaphor of the Möbius strip. Folding critical reflexivity into the process of experiential learning through practices of self-rule is pivotal to advantageously positioning ourselves to begin to learn self-rule through social transition. In order for democratic or any other form of self-government to take hold without becoming a tyranny of the majority, participation needs to be made truly inclusive, and we can do this using the tool of critical pedagogy and andragogy (adult education). As

I hope to elaborate throughout the remainder of this chapter, solidarity and collaborative self-government require our learned ability to think more independently, and empathically. As long as there are internal divisions and hierarchical power relations between people, solidarity remains weak and participatory democracy a hollow and normalized rule of the many. Collaboration should involve informed action from all sources, but it cannot do so in the absence of empathy, which can only come by reflexive questioning of our popular assumptions naturalizing hierarchical relations as inevitable. The ultimate end of critical thinking is the positive transformation of society for the benefit of all through the choices we make through an attendant but undirected expansion of our awareness. New knowledges develop through reflective skepticism, challenging our unexamined assumptions (Anderson, 1996: 22), operating with objectives of collaborative openness and solidarity.

Dolby embraces popular culture as instrumental to the emancipatory collapse of manufactured distinctions between dominant and subordinate classes; but depending upon the content of what is being conveyed, the collapse might well be viewed as an alliance, at least along certain axes of power. The problem I see with introducing popular culture as a pedagogical tool is that it is no more immune to domination than elitist forms of high culture; only the forms of these messages vary. Popular culture forms are altered, while the old biases remain intact. High and low cultures oppose each other but often play by the same rules, inadvertently spreading similarly hierarchical, unexamined presumptions about "human nature." High and low cultures are, in these coincidences, flip sides of the same coin. If such messages are not deconstructed in educational settings, they often become tacitly accepted and the question of employing high or low culture in education becomes rhetorical. Disney's production of *Pocahontas* widely disseminates Pocahontas' story as a fairy tale, reinscribing high culture interpretations of imperial mastery, and minimizing European conquest to a series of romantic discoveries, and avoids much scrutiny, minimized as popular "entertainment." Although this popular interpretation might well be critiqued for diluting high culture, it retains all the key elements, even wrapped within the old Rousseauian designation of the Noble Savage.

When considering popular culture as pedagogy that brings social justice through participatory democracy, we need to examine the issue of inclusivity within mainstream practices. Consider the "stud farm" recently opened by former madam Heidi Fleiss in Nevada.[3] In certain respects, it seems funny and nonsensical to us because within patriarchal heteronormative rule men and women cannot participate in current sexual discourses and practices in equivalent ways. Carole Pateman (1988) suggests that patriarchal power is fundamentally supported by women's sexual availability; and the sex trade as a political relationship with its intrinsic disparities is conveniently attributed to naturalized sex and gender differences, as Anne Fausto-Sterling (2000), Judith Butler (1999), Londa Schiebinger (1993) and Thomas Laqueur (1990) among many others, have shown. Queer and straight women may be afforded opportunities as consumers in the mainstream sex trade; but their participation carries different meanings and they cannot participate in ways that heterosexual men are able to as the normalized standard. Thus, while this opportunity may seem egalitarian in the sense that anyone can formally participate, queer and straight women's attempts at participation only obscure and inadvertently fuel the unjustifiable imbalances. I am not suggesting that women should seek a sense of belonging in the world through equivalent kinds of participation in the sex trade; I use this example to illustrate how important it is to resolve unbalanced baselines of power as raised by the new social movements, so that there can be genuine inclusivity in equal opportunity, without which we cannot unproblematically consider the possibility of participatory democracy, widened through ever-expanding accessibility. Critical thinking skills develop our ability to question normative discourses and imagine useful alternatives, and ultimately, to level the playing field.

Theory and Practice

Dolby justifiably expresses frustration with those who theorize but do little in terms of actual practice. And as I have mentioned, she is not alone; informal educators with the exception of a few, like Paulo Freire, have historically been committed to social transformation through action. Dolby (2003: 271–272, 267–268) discourages critical analysis of "the representations of structural positions" in popular culture, pointing out that interrogating the meaning of texts cannot provide a basis of change. Theory by itself can amount to little more than an exercise for its own sake. It seems to me, however, that transformation requires a three-pronged articulation of practice that is informed as well as informing, where the potential significance of popular culture as emancipatory political terrain would be strengthened with analysis of what is actually being said. I agree with Dolby's observation that popular participation can challenge elitist productions of truth, and by extension, as social constructs knowledges partly depend on structural location and cultural context. Nevertheless, interests do not self-evidently map onto structural positions. The working classes are neither naturally revolutionary, nor inherently passive, and we cannot predict intentions based upon presumed structural interests. In 1858 Engels lamented that the "English proletariat is actually becoming more and more bourgeois" (Stedman-Jones, 1984: 127).

Critical media literacy within education is, for Dolby, needlessly negative, and … "representative of the 'anxiety' half of what McCarthy and his colleagues term the anxiety or celebration approach to the study of popular culture" (Dolby, 2003: 264). Such binaries overlook all the hybrids (almost everything) in between (Latour, 1993). Either/or scenarios reduce us to being either unreservedly in favor of unbounded libertarianism, or risking becoming misanthropes inflicting the dogmatism of our fun-squelching political correctness on others. Political sensitivity has merit, and the importance of fun should be taken seriously; but as thought assessing other thought, assessing other thought, critical thinking need not be anxious, negative, or destructive. Ultimately, the end of critical thinking for Habermas is an emancipatory interest (Anderson, 1996: 168).

In her rejection of theory, Dolby further argues against the efficacy of textual analyses, observing that we cannot predict with certainty how messages will be interpreted; there is "no direct line between the encoded message and the message that individuals receive or decode," and thus it is pointless theorizing them. Dolby argues, for instance, that although romance novels can be detrimental; they have uneven and

contradictory effects, actually offering empowerment along with delete-
riousness to some. Karen Anderson (1996: 160) observes that,

> ... all means of expression used in society have an arbitrary basis ... in North
> America and Europe, shaking the head from side to side indicates no. But in
> certain parts of Africa, it means yes ... because we communicate symbolically,
> there is never a one-to-one correspondence between what is being communi-
> cated and how it might be understood.

Writing on the politics of film, Michael Ryan suggests that we make an
unnecessary and false opposition between culture as a signifying realm,
and society as a prediscursive realm, a world "out there" waiting to
be discovered (Ryan, 1988: 479, 477–486). Ryan argues that social texts
presume existing "social codes of perception that allow it to be received
and decoded by audiences." He advocates textual analysis despite
Dolby's concerns, given that:

> ... formal analysis is inherently social because it is the analysis of represen-
> tational and perceptual conventions that are collectively held and sociologi-
> cal analysis is necessarily formal because film enunciates meaning through
> discursive operations that cannot be deemed secondary to a supposedly extra
> discursive social reality—that reality is constituted and mediated by discourses
> (Ryan, 1988: 478–479).

Anderson reminds us that our presumptions frame what we decipher.
One might point out that a worker in a sweatshop or at Wal-Mart who
assumes he is earning a fair wage would be seen as systematically
exploited by a Marxist theorist. Nevertheless, we still have general codes
and dominant discourses; our presumptions frame what we decipher.
Similarly, "race" may not objectively exist as a self-evident biological
category but it has real effects. In interpreting anything, we "draw heavily on the culturally acceptable perceptions, beliefs, attitudes, and explanations that we all learn in the process of being socialized" (Anderson,
1996: 161), a point to which I return, below.

The problematic nature of objectivity extends to the visual field,
where the act of seeing is mediated by cultural interpretation. Consider
the 1992 Rodney King uprising provoked when a predominantly white
jury acquitted four police officers accused in the beating of Rodney
King. As Judith Butler demonstrates, empirical evidence of videotaped

police violence was mediated by a white episteme, such that King was interpreted as a danger to two dozen white police officers who surrounded him, inflicting nine skull fractures, a concussion, a shattered eye socket and cheekbone, facial nerve damage, a broken leg, and injuries to both knees.[4] In the face of video evidence,

> King is constructed as the origin, intention and object of the selfsame brutality. White police violence is displaced onto King who is reduced to the phantasm of white racist aggression, a phantasm that belongs to white racial aggression as the externalised figure of its own distortion. He becomes, within that schema, nothing other than the site at which that racist violence fears and beats the spectre of its own rage. … if it is *his* violence which impels the causal sequence, and it is his body which receives the blows, then, in effect, he beats himself: he is the beginning and the end of the violence, he brings it on himself (Butler, 1993:20).

Butler argues then, that we can have no "simple recourse to the visible" (Butler, 1993:17) and therefore need to think not just about the event of police brutality, but about its hegemonic context: the attendant "racially saturated field of visibility" (Butler, 1993:15) in which jurors interpreted the video, effortlessly splitting "the violent intention off from the body who wields it and attributes it to the body who receives it" (Butler, 1993:20). The trial demonstrated the impossibility not just of rule of law in the courtroom, but the extension of this to everyday life, where we erroneously assume that we exercise direct, unmediated perception, neutrality and objectivity.

Dominant EuroAmerican discourses are still predominantly patriarchal, heteronormative, white, and middle class. They have been challenged by the new social movements, demonstrating that popular culture is not monolithically unreflexive. We need to become aware of the epistemes we work within to build solidarity. If, as Anderson suggests, we cannot attain a disinterested, objective and neutral perspective because we cannot extricate ourselves from our social and historical locations; if we cannot transcend our specific epistemes, we can still become aware of them and use this awareness to imaginatively generate alternative discourses (Anderson, 1996: 170).

In her final bid to argue for the importance of practice over theory, Dolby expresses resignation over hierarchical domination exercised amongst the multitude, conceding to an interpretation of its natural inevitability as a source of pleasure that human desire is inexorably drawn to:

> [d]espite the visceral appeal of critical media studies, it is unrealistic to expect that youth will reject popular culture because of its commercial nature, or its potentially racist, sexist, violent, or homophobic content. As Grossberg reminds us, popular culture is a source of pleasure and human desire for pleasure will always draw us back to it, despite our intellectual critiques (Dolby, 2003: 264).

The implication that oppressive practices are a matter of natural human desires is an erroneous proposition precluding social change. When we reject the naturalness and inevitability of events, a space is opened for the emergence of alternative possibilities. This is crucial for any analysis of human agency within popular culture, allowing us to assess how unconstrained (free) our choices are within it and, by extension, how inclusive a space it can offer. Dolby (2003: 280) weakens her central emancipatory claim with her claim that, "the 'discovery' of racism, sexism, and other forms of oppression in popular culture is no longer news, and it appears that critique is doing little to actually change that reality." Ultimately, along with other advocates of popular culture as pedagogical method, she strives for an inclusive democracy—as opposed to the "current sham of democracy that merely legitimates authority through electoral mechanisms" (Hardt, 2007: xix)—through the inclusion of the masses in education through the addition of popular culture to the curriculum. But in her efforts to demonstrate the emancipatory merits of mainstream culture Dolby overlooks the pivotal question of popular collusion with elitist discourses, and we are left to assume either that oppressive practices are natural and inevitable, such that we had best settle for small reforms, or that under the auspices of popular culture deemed essentially "good," social inequality will somehow work itself out in the proverbial wash.

I have argued thus far that theoretical analysis must work in concert with political practice to achieve inclusive participation in democratic education. Historically, where democracies have flourished, minorities have not. The marginalized Other within contemporary Western popular culture remain silent and socially invisible, if in some cases marked (and sometimes apprehended) by their status as "visible minorities" (Bannerji, 1993). Robyn Wiegman (1995) identifies "Western economies of visibility" as informed by a privileged sense of vision within modernist scientific discourses. These systems accommodate hierarchies whereby the Self as the paradoxically invisible, but universal standard enjoys disproportionate entitlement linked to such statuses as race, gender, sexuality, and class.

Popular culture purportedly extends to everyone a voice, cultivating social equality. Those who rise to popularity with a salient voice often speak to norms in a circular fashion. Normalizing discourses (ideas and ways of talking to and about each other, and of making judgments about what is normal or self-evident) against which notions of alterity, pathology, and criminality are formed, limit the autonomy of our choices of what to think, and what we can effectively or legitimately give voice to. In addition to the incorporation of popular culture in education, we need to reduce rote, surface learning, and encourage more in-depth problem solving skills and critical analysis.

Because popular culture is driven by private commercial interests and marketized entrepreneurialism, consumer driven global market mechanisms are systematically replacing state governance under neoliberal policies, negating even the heuristic value of binary divisions between state and civil society (Garland, 2006: 363). Popular culture cultivates burgeoning spaces for liberatory expression, and much popular culture moves beyond the mainstream. It is hardly monolithic, but marginalization and silencing abound. Circumscribed by questions of commercial profitability, exceptional ideas often lose their edge once adopted. Rap music is a case in point. The commercialism that operates within neoliberalism tends to co-opt and neutralize that which may originally have been politically radical. Alternatively, rap music would not have been co-opted in the first place if it was too radically different. Still, a wider range exists of what is being said even in the last thirty years. Through commercialism, artists of African descent might profit from mainstream culture; yet, rap music sometimes follows the self-deprecation of historical blackface minstrel shows; but despite the commercialism, elements of the subversive thrive.[5] It is also possible, as Mark Ryan (1988) points out, that popular culture texts might align themselves with dominant discourses, but also convey energies that potentially disturb the status quo. Again, popular culture is complicated and uneven. Nevertheless, there are barely acknowledged voices on the margins, contributing to a diminishing of the potential multiplicity of discursivity, which comes to speak to market driven norms, along with the atrophy of Other voices that comes from their delegitimization, a marginalizing process complicated by the general presumption of freedom of expression. How does the mainstream gain legitimacy?

Agency and Hegemony

Popular texts can maneuver consent into different directions. Educators who adopt the Gramscian concept of hegemony seek to explore how popular culture as a vehicle functions as a central "arena of struggle for consent" wherein the dominant classes win rather than force the consent of the subordinated (Dolby, 2003: 262–263). Within education, they envision a struggle over the issue of either allowing the progressive atrophy of an increasingly meaningless educational system or preferably reviving and extending education by struggling against the elitism of high culture, partly fortified by inaccessible texts. Relativist social theorists would agree that people have agency, but raise three central concerns about the concept of hegemony within the social control model. First, as a paradigm conveying the notion of absolute, top-down domination, social control leaves very little room for agency. Michel Foucault declares that "there is no binary and all-encompassing opposition between rulers and ruled at the root of power relations" (Bristow, 1977: 177). This is not to deny domination and resistance, but to propose that power is not exercised in a single, linear, downward vector. It can be constitutive as well as repressive.

Second, hegemony refers mainly to class consciousness. The new social movements constitute a multiplicity of voices of dissent from producers of low and high culture, neither of which are monolithic unities. Ernesto Laclau and Chantal Mouffe's (1985) concept of radical democracy involves the displacement of the economic reductionism of the Marxist base-superstructure model, with its prioritization of class over all other relationships, by such new social movements as queer sexualities, antiracism, feminisms, and disability activism. Third, the application of hegemony to popular culture is valuable for raising the issue of politicization, but risks a reading of ideological domination and false consciousness that suggests that we drift aimlessly "through a banal existence of consumption, obedience, and propaganda" (Boje, 2000). Reductionist explanations of the social control looming in an increasingly powerful state overlook contemporary forms of social power, the objectives and techniques of which are multifarious and diverse (Garland, 2006: 363). Moreover, common objectives may come from unaffiliated interest groups, as exemplified by the support of some feminist groups for choice, in keeping with the advocacy of this by various groups of men who would consider themselves unsympathetic to feminist concerns (Valverde and Weir, 2006: 82). Whereas many Marxists would claim that the media is conscientiously used by dominant groups to obscure actual reality, post-structuralist accounts would argue that at least some of the parameters defining current affairs are immediately, at least, largely invisible to everyone (Green, 2007). According to David Garland (2006: 363), authorities are generally candid when they express concern over issues of protection against crime: "Social policy objectives ... are usually just what they say and not some devious cover for capitalist class interests, the reproduction of patriarchy, or some other system-function." Nevertheless, their analyses may be based on inaccurate information and moral panics. Unstable and never absolute as an all-encompassing pressure, power is exercised everywhere unpredictably, in a whole array of interconnected relationships. Popular culture is a significant venue for the agency of social groups in the context of liberal democratic states, which unlike fascist states, must dispense with direct forms of constraint on people's identities (Valverde and Weir, 2006: 82).

Dismissing mass culture as manipulative and stupefying, Adorno contends that it "impedes the development of autonomous, independent individuals who judge and decide consciously for themselves" (Dolby, 2003: 261). Messages can become ingrained, but they can also lose their power through repetition and habituation. Nonetheless, some messages become normalized and it is difficult to deconstruct them, even if we argue against the notion of people as passive recipients of information generated by mainstream culture. We make choices within a limited framework constrained by the discursive boundaries of what we can imagine (Anderson, 1996: 28). Change comes with an expansion of the interpretive possibilities. Furthermore, we relate to modern forms of power not as coerced or deceived subjects within a state-based model of social control over civil society, but as individuals with agency, whose identities are wrought through active and uneven engagement with diverse and scattered governing bodies, as well as through vigilant self-regulation (Garland, 2006: 363). The key insight of Foucault's theme of governmentality is that the omnipotent state is not set over against civil society, and institutions do not govern us independently of ourselves; rather, it is *we* who self-regulate, vigilantly monitoring our own and others' conduct through everyday actions and the smallest gestures in "a complex web of capillary relations of power" (Day, 2005: 124). Given all these variations and complexities, we can eliminate menacing hegemonic ruling class conspiracies, and even any unified set of norms (Valverde and Weir, 2006: 82; Garland, 2006: 363).

Governmentality

Particularly useful in analyses of power as constitutive rather than simply repressive, the governmentality literature can offer a more refined tool than hegemony for thinking about how we manage our own conduct and that of others, how we are governed within current neoliberal policies, and how we exercise agency through the interpretation and management of social issues and interaction within the global market. Governmentality refers to *technologies of self*, our strict self-regulation involving identity development and alignment to social ideals in accordance with expert advice we seek; and *forms of rule*, by which various authorities manage populations. Scholarship on governmentality problematizes the turn from the welfare state to postmodern capitalism, analyzing how various ways of exercising power depends on rationalities, modes of conduct, as well as on identity formation and the management of populations (Garland, 2006: 357–358).

Historical or genealogical analysis can shed light on the ways in which discourses become normalized and naturalized. For instance, scientific constructions of sex and gender have historically naturalized sociobiological themes of gender antagonism that persist in currently popular expert discourses like John Gray's, *Men are From Mars, Women are From Venus*. In this case, the power relations tied to conventional gender relationships exist not because men are men and women are women, but because they are part of a historical moment that has produced discursive binaries specific to our sociohistorical, cultural, political, and economic contexts. Normalization produces self-regulating individuals, where naturalized relationships and behaviors commonly but inaccurately attributed to human nature contribute to the constitution of identities and perceptions of deviance and criminality. Arguably, for instance, gender-based identities are performative habits, no more than "a set of repeated acts within a highly rigid regulatory frame that congeal over time to produce the appearance of substance, of a natural sort of being" (Butler, 1990: 33).

The media industry breeds normalization, in its exercise of power about what can be legitimately said through decisions about what is reported, as Edward Said's (1998) discussion of Orientalism aptly demonstrates. Power can create knowledge in the sense that institutions authorized to do so determine the conditions under which statements come to be counted as true or false (Hacking, 1986). Foucault's ideas about the imbricated processes of power and knowledge are germane to the issues of inclusion and agency within popular culture in education in that knowledge is transmitted by normalizing discourses and practices, informing and setting parameters around what we can legitimately choose to express. Certainly, we may choose to behave outside the bounds of the acceptable within liberal democracies, but may put ourselves on the defensive in the process. Garland (2006: 363, 372–273) distinguishes freedom (as unrestrained choice of actions) from agency (as the capacity for decision-based action), observing that neoliberal techniques of government require increased individual agency, without an attendant increase in individual freedom of choice. We may choose then, but only within certain parameters of what we collectively deem legitimate.

Discourses confine us, and we additionally subjugate ourselves through seemingly autonomous choices informed by normative knowledges generated by disciplines such as science, medicine, psychology, and psychiatry. Foucauldians would argue that governing bodies exercising "power/knowledge"—whether the media industry, experts, or a myriad of others historically and in the present–contribute to the organization of our understandings of such concepts as "madness," "the homosexual," "the criminal type," "sexuality," "the delinquent," or "the disciplined employee." The self-awareness that we struggle to develop through "working on" ourselves or our relationships then, is a form of self-surveillance; a productive, disciplinary power we internalize and practice rigorously and perpetually. Choosing to actively participate in the cultivation of our own identities, we engage modern forms of power as constitutive rather than simply repressive forces (Foucault, 1977: 194). Under postmodern capitalism we align our subjectivities with such identities as good citizens, consumers, or entrepreneurs. We are not unfree, but our freedom defined as unbridled choices of actions, is limited compared to our agency linked to decision-based action (Garland, 2006: 372–373).

Connected to this, moral regulation studies are typically framed within studies of governmentality. Moral regulation refers to the processes by which some behaviors, ideals, and values are marginalized and proscribed while others are legitimized and naturalized. In the United States, the concept of discrimination is an anathema to the American Dream; yet the prevalence of systemic inequalities and structural violence against people within a polity espousing democratic equality is undeniable. Moral regulation persists through the paradox that, for instance, although we may know that someone is being discriminated against, our collective belief is that in liberal democracies everyone has an equal chance, brought into fruition by the cultivation of good character and moral self-government. Our struggles become inwardly focused as we reason that if the thrifty are able to attain the American Dream, we have no one to blame but ourselves for failing to prosper.

These ways of knowing and exercising power organize what we consider to be self-evident whether conveyed through high or low culture. All texts, from those on opera or law to those on popular film, are cultural constructs embodying values and aspirations pertaining to what constitute our truths about all aspects, from happiness, beauty, and childhood, to responsibility, "wellness," "healthy relationships," and sexuality. It is in this sense that reality is constructed, not simply discovered. Events happen, but we interpret their meaning according to what we believe to be true at any particular historical moment and cultural context, these interpretations being constrained within the discursive boundaries of what we can imagine (Anderson, 1996: 28).

Though not passive subjects, in certain respects we have become variously anaesthetized and habituated to normalized passivity. In keeping with Spinoza, Hardt (2007: xvi) observes that, "if the population is ignorant and superstitious then establishing democracy would merely mean instituting the rule of ignorance and superstition." There is nothing essentially emancipatory about mainstream popular culture, nor anything inherently inclusive about democratic participation. Again, it is up to us to make it so.

Getting from here to there:
Informed and Informative Practice

Change is possible. The Implicit Association Test, developed by Harvard's "Project Implicit" analyzes our automatic stereotyping attitudes, demonstrating that test scores improve after we have had repetitive exposure to interpretations that counter our prevailing attitudes; experiences that challenge us to see differently. We can actively change our prejudices, learning to become aware of how they affect our judgments and actions.[6]

But how can we begin to generate the positive social change that Dolby and other informal educators envision in light of self-defeating discourses that naturalize antagonistic and divisive hierarchical relationships, attempted democratic practice on uneven ground, commercialization and neutralization of fresh ideas, agency limited by the constraints of what we can imagine, as well as overarching transnational oppression within a neoliberal context? Nothing is absolute, simple, or evenly developed.

The question of how to carry out social change towards a new and liberatory framework constitutes the major impasse of the modern revolutionary tradition (Hardt, 2007: ix). Lamenting what they see as widespread under-education, many on the Left have advocated top-down models of social transformation directed by intellectual elites. (Ryan, 1988: 477–478). Social democrats tending to perceive humanity as naturally only responsive to rule from above, advocate the preservation of state management (Hardt, 2007: ix). But bottom-up models are currently advocated by those who question the whole premise of an essential human nature, arguing in any case that the state thwarts human liberation, and should be replaced by active self-rule through a bottom-up approach—positive social change by and for autonomous groups within the multitude (Hardt, 2007). Those who reject top-down transformation object to external guidance from intellectuals as undemocratic. Hardt (2007: xx) suggests that:

> … it makes no sense for the transition to be ruled over by a hegemonic figure, whether that be a dictatorship of the proletariat or any other force that stands above or transcends the multitude. How could democracy, after all, result from its opposite?

Laclau argues for the need of a hegemonic figure positioned above the social field offering guidance, thereby fulfilling the party function, but within a "failed transcendence"—without actually being the party (Hardt, 2007: xvii). Neither state-run nor privately funded, non-directive, critical pedagogy and andragogy could serve as a way to bridge the gap between top-down and bottom-up approaches, as an action-oriented tool that enhances our independent thinking skills, enabling informed practice along with the experiential learning that comes only through practice that Hardt (2007) advocates. We need to develop the necessary subjectivities to govern ourselves, and as I see it, social transformation requires an articulation of practice that is both informed and experientially informing.

The dilemma of education and practice presents a chicken-and-egg question of where to begin; but the starting point may not matter, since change is uneven. We could set about moving in liberatory directions, jumping onto various expanding collaborative movements of revolutionary change. The question of what motivates people to think and to act has numerous possible answers. Laclau sees the articulation of vocal demands forming a sequence of initiatives around bread and butter issues, as well as "for rights or services or freedoms;" a plurality of demands through which emerges widespread popular collaboration and social transformation (Hardt, 2007: xvii). These articulations could be facilitated through a revolutionary approach to critical education.

Critical Thinking and the Sociological Imagination

The ultimate end of critical thinking is positive transformation for the benefit of all through self-directed expansion of our awareness and choices. Critical thinking does not imply top-down directives; instead it facilitates active autonomous collaboration through individual and collective reflection based on "reasonable reflective thinking focused on deciding what to believe or do" (Anderson, 1996: 22). With the sharpening of our critical thinking skills we can expand the array of legitimate choices we have, by examining and questioning our normalized assumptions.

People within mainstream EuroAmerican cultures are habituated to noncollaborative hierarchical relations between social groups that the new social movements have formed responses to. Popular culture currently assumes a standard of things such as whiteness, able-bodiedness, patriarchy, heteronormativity, and middle-class values. These currently dominant discourses need to be empathically deconstructed, not to breed homogeneity, but rather increased awareness about antagonistic relationships. Michael Hardt (2005) recalls Audre Lorde's observation that "our differences are our strength" and following the antiracist slogan, "We don't want a world without race; we want a world in which race doesn't matter," Hardt suggests that, "We don't want a world without difference. We want a world with difference; but we want a world in which difference doesn't imply hierarchy." We need to be mindful of the myriad, contradictory and changeable ways that power is exercised within popular culture, collectively guiding the production of our cultural expressions within truly inclusive education. Emancipatory change on a global revolutionary scale needs to come about in the—however, uneven—process of abolishing all relationships based on hierarchy and domination.

Coalescence needs to begin with Weber's concept of *verstehen*, of empathy generated by people through self-directed learning processes guided instrumentally by critical thought. Not unlike Hardt (2005), Freire advocates respectful and empathetic, "profound love for the world and for people" as a foundation for dialogue and collaboration generating acts of freedom. Only then can people begin to participate on even ground. Education could be a site that nurtures the new social movements, a space for deconstructing relationships that unilaterally prevent nonhierarchical difference and full participation within democratic and other collaborative approaches.

If we are confined by the limits of entertaining what we imagine, it follows that through the cultivation of what C. Wright Mills coined as the "sociological imagination" we can not only contextualize events, but also construct alternative knowledges through inventiveness, breaking away from conventional understandings of everyday life. Creative thought can shed new light onto what we have come to accept as inevitable through a kind of reverse culture shock; imagining nonsensical reversals and ludicrous scenarios and then inquiring why these seem absurd. Such exercises can help to deepen our understanding of obscure connections, aiding in the deconstruction of hierarchical relationships. (Anderson, 1996: 24, 26, 28, 34).

German philosophy and the writings of Marx and Engels in particular generated the critical approach to knowledge, but for Mills it involves the cultivation of what we can imagine, questioning what is legitimatized and justified reflecting on our acquired beliefs. As such, critical thinking is an ultimately emancipatory exercise (Anderson, 1996: 168), giving us tools to envision alternative ways of being.

Thomas Jefferson suggested that revolutionary social transformation should be an ongoing process, marked differentially by each generation (Hardt, 2007: xi). Abandoning notions of discovery of universal and self-evident Truth, critical thinkers develop tolerance for uncertainty, with the understanding that knowledge claims are provisional. New knowledges develop through reflective skepticism, challenging our unexamined assumptions, operating with objectives of collaborative openness and solidarity. Within critical theory, the nurturing of alternative ways of seeing through ongoing re-evaluation of social directions is a process that by definition poses periodic challenges to knowledge bases, drawing on numerous sources, and examining all premises as relative, socially constructed claims (Anderson, 1996: 22, 28, 30, 190–191). Rather than seeking one correct answer, critical analyses pursue diverse interpretations of events rejecting the possibility of "an objectively neutral or disinterested perspective," while inviting investigation of how standards are formed and choices are made between differing perspectives (Anderson, 1996: 27–8, 170).

Workspaces for Self-Informed Practice

Following Paulo Freire's (1972) sentiment that too often, formal and conservative curriculum-based education is disconnected and alienating rhetoric, Paul Willis approvingly predicts the withering away of formal education, and its replacement by informal education through popular culture as a more meaningful experience:

> ... in so far as educational practices are still predicated on traditional liberal humanist lines and on the assumed superiority of high art, they will become almost totally irrelevant to the real energies and interests of most young people and have no part in their identity formation. Common culture will, increasingly, undertake, in its own ways, the roles that education has vacated (Dolby, 2003: 264).

Advocating educational reforms through small-scale resistance against neoliberal power, Dolby (2003: 276) maintains that "The threats to its future must be met with resistance and a firm commitment to democratic public schooling that ensures equality of access and opportunity." I agree with Dolby contra Willis that educational institutions are important as formal workspaces. As public institutions, schools, already in place, could provide potentially revolutionary local spaces for popular, bottom-up collaboration amongst every age group. As members of the multitude we could storm the bastions of state educational institutions, making them their own and fundamentally changing their structure to cultivate considered independent thought. We would assume informed stewardship over schools as a means of production of truth, learning the ropes of this stewardship as we go. Education could be fundamentally transformed to become a more useful exercise of deep as opposed to surface learning, melding critical thinking skills that require concerted efforts of reflexive analysis along with the accessibility of expansive popular culture.

We could nurture openness to intellectual curiosity, problem solving and relevant learning, rather than have the undemocratic imposition of rote learning of subject matter units that rarely motivate learners beyond grades competition.

Change comes through the expansion of interpretive possibilities. This involves openness to marginal voices, and to questioning constructions of normalcy as well as naturalized discourses that justify social hierarchies. If we are limited by what we can imagine, and with normalization dampening the voices at the margins, it follows that we should consider unconventional ideas of those who could potentially offer interesting alternatives. Angela Davis' recent work (2003) on prisons is illustrative. Where some would accept the proviso separating the guilty from the innocent, they might also understand that society should respect what is human in the guilty and would seek the provision of amenities. Davis rejects penal reforms that would extend the visiting rights of prisoners or to outfit their cells with flush toilets, turning instead to questions of the deep social and moral division between innocence and guilt, the normal and the pathological, good and evil. Davis' work demonstrates our media amplified fears of criminals, in keeping with Foucault's observation that we "brandish the threat of the monstrous so as to reinforce the ideology of good and evil, of the things that are permitted and prohibited."[7] Following Davis, we might ask why the kind of crime our media focuses on is street crime rather than white collar, environmental, or corporate crime. We might ask how people are selected and excluded in the name of the "normal individual."

Dolby's call for the incorporation of popular culture into education indicates a desire for liberatory change and accessible learning on the part of an increasing number of educators; but popular culture, engaged in uncritically–whether inside or beyond the institutionalized education—will not function automatically as an inclusive pedagogical site, challenging elitist exclusivity. We need to be mindful of the myriad, contradictory and changeable ways that power is exercised within popular culture to make our attempts at inclusivity more effective. This requires a dismantling of the theory vs. practice binary, with attention to theory as inseparable from practice. Although it is important to employ popular culture along with equally valuable difficult texts to explain ideas, pedagogy could more effectively improve social conditions with educational initiatives that we might learn from through our practice, but which are also informed before being put into practice.

Traditional, state-run education may be becoming obsolete in the wake of popular culture. Educational institutions, reflecting both high and low culture, could become workspaces (where self-regulation is turned to autonomy and genuine, considered, freedom of expression) that participants might freely use as a commonly run site for self-directed creative collaboration through the honing of critical thinking skills, thereby fostering independent thought and empathic exchange. The current pedagogical crisis provides an opportunity to strive for more than "teachable moments," because the end of education could be revolutionary.

Notes

1. On the term "visible minority, " and its constructed peculiarity and ascribed status of visibility despite overall invisibility, see Himani Bannerji (1993). Eric Wolf (1982: 76) suggests that "most of the societies studied by anthropologists are an outgrowth of the expansion of Europe and not the pristine precipitates of past evolutionary stages." European imperial expansion encountered cultures having long and intricate histories; yet "a complex orchestration of antagonistic forces is celebrated instead as the unfolding of a timeless essence" and imperialist expansion is defended as benevolent and necessary, obfuscating wars, slavery persecution and the possibility of other historical outcomes (Wolf, 1982: 5–6).

2. I use the term "multitude" in keeping with Michael Hardt and Antonio Negri's articulation of it, following Spinoza's *multitudo*. "Multitude" refers to current social subjects as a heterogeneous multiplicity; an "inconclusive constituent relation" in contrast to "the people," a term that denotes a unified, single will, "a constituted synthesis that is prepared for sovereignty" (Hardt and Negri, 2000: 103).

3. http://www.guardian.co.uk/frontpage/story/0,16518,1645555,00.html
4. http://prop1.org/legal/prisons/kinga2.htm (accessed 26 October 2007).
5. I am grateful to Kelvin Sealey and Andrew Dubois for their comments pertaining to this example.
6. "Project Implicit." https://implicit.harvard.edu/implicit/
7. Quoted from "Revolutionary Action: Until Now" A Discussion with Michel Foucault http://info.interactivist.net/article.pl?sid=03/01/22/1544248

References

Anderson, Karen. 1996. *Sociology: A Critical Introduction.* Nelson, Canada: Scarborough.

Bannerji, Himani. 1993. "Popular Images of South Asian Women," in Himani Bannerji, ed., *Returning the Gaze: Essays on Feminism, Racism and Politics* (pp. 144–152). Toronto: Sister Vision Press.

Bristow, Joseph. 1997. *Sexuality.* London: Routledge.

Butler, Judith. 1993. "Endangerer/Endangering: Schematic Racism and White Paranoia," in Robert Gooding Williams, ed., *Reading Rodney King/Reading Urban Uprising* (pp. 15–22). New York: Routledge.

______ *Gender Trouble: Feminism and the Subversion of Identity.* New York: Routledge, 1990.

Davis, Angela. 2003. *Are Prisons Obsolete?* New York: Seven Stories.

Day, Richard. 2005. *Gramsci Is Dead: Anarchist Currents in the Newest Social Movements.* Toronto: Between the Lines,

Dolby, Nadine. Fall 2003. "Popular Culture and Democratic Practice," *Harvard Educational Review,* 73(3) 258–284.

Edward Said: On Orientalism. (1998) Produced & edited by Sanjay Talreja. Executive Producer, Director & Editor Sut Jhally.

Foucault, Michel. 1977. *Discipline and Punish: The Birth of the Prison,* A. Sheridan, trans, Harmondsworth: Peregrine.

Freire, Paulo. 1972. *Pedagogy of the Oppressed.* Harmondsworth: Penguin.

Garland, David. 2006. "'Governmentality' and the Problem of Crime: Foucault, Criminology, Sociology," *Theoretical Criminology* 1(2). Sage Publications, 1997. Reprinted in Amanda Glasbeek, ed., *Moral Regulation and Governance in Canada,* (pp. 357–385). Toronto: Canadian Scholars' Press.

Gray, John. 1992. *Men are From Mars, Women are From Venus.* New York: Harper Collins.

Hacking, Ian. 1986. "The Archaeology of Knowledge," in D. Couzens Hoy, ed., *Foucault: A Critical Reader.* New York: Basil Blackwell.

Hardt, Michael. 2007. *Michael Hardt Presents Thomas Jefferson: The Declaration of Independence.* London: Verso.

______ & Antoni Negri. 2000. *Empire.* Cambridge: Harvard University Press.

Jones, Gareth Stedman. Autumn 1984. "Some Notes on Karl Marx and the English Labour Movement," *History Workshop Journal*, 18.

Laclau, Ernesto & Chantal Mouffe. 1985. *Hegemony and Socialist Strategy: Towards a Radical, Democratic Politics*. London: Verso.

Laqueur, Thomas. 1990. *Making Sex: Body and Gender from the Greeks to Freud*. Cambridge: Harvard University Press.

Latour, Bruno. 1993. *We Have Never Been Modern*. Cambridge: Harvard University Press.

McClintock, Anne. 1995. *Imperial Leather: Race, Gender, and Sexuality in the Colonial Contest*. New York: Routledge.

Montrose, Louis. 1991. "The Work of Gender in the Discourse of Discovery," *Representations*, Winter (33) (pp. 1–41).

Pateman, Carole. 1988. *The Sexual Contract*. Stanford: Stanford University Press.

Rose, Nikolas. 1990. *Governing the Soul: The Shaping of the Private Self*. London: Routledge.

Ryan, Michael. 1988. "The Politics of Film: Discourse, Psychoanalysis, Ideology," In *Marxism and the Interpretation of Culture* (pp. 477–486). Chicago: University of Illinois Press.

Schiebinger, Londa. 1993. *Nature's Body: Gender in the Making of Modern Science*. Boston: Beacon Press.

Shohat, Ella & Robert Stam. 1994. *Unthinking Eurocentrism: Multiculturalism and the Media*. New York: Routledge.

Spurr, David. 1993. *The Rhetoric of Empire: Colonial Discourse in Journalism, Travel Writing and Imperial Administration*. Durham: Duke University Press.

Wiegman, Robyn. 1995. *American Anatomies: Theorizing Race and Gender*. Durham: Duke University Press.

Wolf, Eric. 1982. *Europe and the People without History*. Berkeley: University of California Press.

Valverde, Mariana & Lorna Weir, 1988. "The Struggles of the Immoral: Preliminary Remarks on Moral Regulation," *Resources for Feminist Research* 17(3). Ontario Institute for Studies in Education, University of Toronto. Reprinted in Amanda Glasbeek, ed., 2006. *Moral Regulation and Governance in Canada*. Toronto: Canadian Scholars' Press.

Websites

Boje, David. March 8, 2000. Panoptic & Hegemonic Stories. http://business.nmsu.edu/~dboje/panoptic.html (accessed June 2006).

Green, Steven. "How can some of Foucault's ideas and perspectives be usefully applied to the study of the mass media in society?" http://www.theory.org.uk/f-essay1.htm (accessed June 8, 2006).

Michael Hardt at European Graduate School EGS 2005. http://www.youtube.com/
    watch?v=bc4pP96suIE (accessed October 26, 2007).
"Project Implicit." https://implicit.harvard.edu/implicit/ (accessed June 2006).
"Revolutionary Action: Until Now" A Discussion with Michel Foucault. Interactivist
    Info Exchange Collaborative Authorship, Collective Intelligence. http://info.
    interactivist.net/; http://info.interactivist.net/article.pl?sid=03/01/22/1544248
    (accessed August 2006).

Chapter Three

Mode of Address: It's a Film Thing

ELIZABETH ELLSWORTH

I didn't study the field of education in graduate school. I studied movies. Hollywood movies, mostly. But because I was a teaching assistant from the first day of grad school, I was also trying to figure out how to teach. Most days in grad school, I would watch a movie like *Young Mr. Lincoln* or *Meet Me in St. Louis*. I would read and try to "get" Althusser or Lacan or Eisenstein or Kuhn or Mulvey or Barthes—folks who wrote about images and stories and meaning and desire and social change. I would try to teach a discussion section of undergraduate students how to analyze the form, style, genre, and ideology of the film they had just seen. And I would be fascinated and reinvigorated by the social, political, and aesthetic power of the movies.

I got hired out of communication arts and into a school of education to teach video production and media criticism for educators. It's been a cross-cultural experience. I didn't speak the language of educational research. I didn't know the stories or characters of the field.

Most alien and alienating of all was having to learn the theories and practices of this new academic world called "curriculum and instruction" in the complete absence of suspense, romance, seduction, visual pleasure, music, plot, humor, tap dancing, or pathos. Everything I had learned about contemporary theories of linguistics, literary criticism, semiotics, feminism, and culture was learned in the presence of—in the light of, in the pleasure of, in the wake of—some movie's story, metaphors, stars, images, and mode of address.

But education wasn't like the communication arts of film or television. It wasn't in the humanities. It was more like the sociology classes I took—the ones taught through programmed workbook textbooks. The field of education was, I found out, a social science.

What I've learned most from my decade-long encounter with education as an academic field is, I don't want to teach or learn in the absence of pleasure, plot, moving and being moved, metaphor, cultural artifacts, audience engagement and interaction.

That's where mode of address comes in. It's been 20 years since I started working as a teaching assistant in an introduction to film course. I'm 14 years into trying to figure out what people think they're doing in this academic field of education and why they've made that field into what it appears to be. And I'm thinking again about modes of address.

Mode of Address in Film Studies

Mode of address is a film studies term with a lot of theoretical and political baggage attached to it. I learned about it in classes on film and social change. What it boils down to is this question: Who does this film think you are?

Here is a selective reading of some of the theory and politics behind this question, and behind the concept of mode of address. I'm not interested in trying to define exactly what mode of address is through this revisit to my academic roots. I'm interested in why, when I think as an educator about pedagogy these days, I keep thinking about it in terms of mode of address. I'm wondering how educators might in turn be educated by encounters with various notions of mode of address, including the one in film studies.

Film theorists have developed the notion of mode of address to deal, in a film-specific way, with some huge questions that cut across film studies, literary and art criticism, sociology, anthropology, history, and education. Those questions have to do with the relation between "the social" and "the individual." Questions like, What is the relation between a film's text and a spectator's experience? A novel's structure and a reader's interpretation? A painting and a viewer's emotion? A social practice and cultural identity? A curriculum and learning? What is the relation, in other words, between the "outside" of society and the "inside" of the human psyche? How can it be equally true that "people act in self-directed and intentional ways," and yet, the patterns that inform their actions—how they think, what they "see," what they desire—"are already aspects of social being" (Donald, 1991, p. 2)?

These are big questions. They're also key for people interested in social change. Once you figure out the relationship between a film's text and a spectator's experience, for example, you might be able to change or influence, even control, a spectator's response by designing a film in a particular way. Or, you may be able to teach viewers how to resist or subvert who a film thinks they are, or wants them to be.

For over 25 years, film theorists have been using the notion of mode of address, in some form or other, to grapple with these issues. Here, I'm going to trace some of the meanings that this notion has had for film theorists. This selective reading starts with mode of address as a concept that refers to something that is "in" a film's text, which then somehow acts on its imagined or real viewers or both. Then there's a moment in the logic of film theory when some film theorists begin to see mode of address less as something that is in a film and more as an event that takes place somewhere *between* the social and the individual. Here, the event of address takes place in the space that is social, psychic, or both, between the film's text and the viewers' uses of it. This shift from locating mode of address inside a film's text to understanding it as an event will propel my selective reading of mode of address out of film theory and into education, cultural studies, and psychoanalysis.

Who Does This Film Think You Are?

Films, like letters, books, or television commercials, are *for* someone. They have intended and imagined audiences. Now, film directors, scriptwriters, studio producers, and theater owners are often far removed from "real" or "actual" moviegoers. The distances can be economic, temporal, social, geographical, ideological, gendered, raced. In addition, films go through many alterations between script and screening. Yet most decisions about a film's narrative structure, "look," and packaging are made in light of conscious and unconscious assumptions about "who" its audiences "are," what they want, how they read films, which films they'll pay to see next year, what makes them laugh or cry, what they fear, and who they think they are in relation to themselves, to others, and to the social and cultural passions and tensions of the day.

Films have intended and imagined audiences. They also have desired audiences. Some films, like *Jurassic Park*, are produced with the desire to attract the largest possible "mass" (worldwide) audience. Others, like *Go Fish*, are produced to appeal to the people who go to the Sundance Film Festival and are made with the hope of getting bookings in small hip urban "art" theaters attended by people on ideological, sexual, racial, and political fringes.

The concept of mode of address is built on this contention: In order for a film to work for an audience, in order for it to simply make sense to a viewer, or make her laugh, root for a character, suspend her disbelief, cry, scream, feel satisfied at the end—the viewer must enter into a particular relationship with the film's story and image system.

Here is one way to conceptualize this process: There is a seat in the movie theater to which the movie screen "points," a seat for which the cinematographic effects and frame compositions were designed, a seat at which the lines of perspective converge—giving the fullest illusion of depth, movement, "reality." It's from that physical position that the film looks the best. Likewise, there is a "position" within power relations and interests, within gender and racial constructions, within knowledge, to which the film's story and visual pleasure is addressed. It's from that "subjective position" that the film's assumptions about who the audience is work with the least effort, contradiction, or slippage.

For example, films intended for 12-year-old white boys who live in the suburbs are pitched to the positions that such boys are assumed to occupy (or desired to occupy by producers of films and spin-off merchandisers) within contemporary social relations, market tastes, sexual fantasy and desire, gender, and racial construction. In order for those boys to "catch" the film and run with it, they have to be in the place that the film is pitched to. In order for them to become part of the structure of relations that make up the system of looks, desires, pleasures, expectations, narrative setups and payoffs that make up the film-going experience, they have to be there. In order for them to "complete" the film as its producers hoped they would complete it, they have to assume the positions offered in those systems—at least for the length of the film, at least imaginatively.

"Hey, You!"

Thus, filmmakers make many conscious and unconscious assumptions and wishes about the who that their film is addressed to and the social positions and identities that their audience is occupying. And those assumptions and desires leave intended and unintended traces in the film itself. To some schools of film study, a film is composed, then, not only of a system of images and an unfolding story. It is also composed of a structure of address to an imagined audience.

The "traces" of this structure aren't visible. They don't offer themselves up for study on the screen like aspects of a film's style, such as composition of objects and people in the frame, use of color, movement, editing, lighting, and so on. A film's mode of address is more like the film's narrative structure than its image system. Like story or plot, mode of address is not visible.

Nor does someone in the film literally say: "Hey, you! You 12-year-old white suburban boy! Watch this! It'll be fun. And you'll want to buy the toy. And you'll feel older and more powerful—and taller—than you are and the whole world will seem to be centered around you. And when the film ends, you'll feel that being a white American suburban 12-year-old boy is the best thing in the world to be." Not a literal visual or spoken moment, mode of address is a structuring of the relationships between the film and its viewers that unfolds over time.

Film scholars who have focused on mode of address have come up with ways of talking about this invisible process of "hailing" a viewer into a position from which to read the film. Critics who study film narrative have borrowed concepts from literary criticism and theater and invented others so that they can name and analyze the intangible experience of story on film. These include plot, character, subtext, genre, causal links, point of view, and so on. Similarly, critics interested in mode of address have come up with concepts that name and analyze aspects of their ideas about being hailed. "Audience positioning" is one of them. Masterman (1985) describes it this way:

> [W]ithin the visual media, we, as audience members, are compelled to occupy a particular *physical* position by virtue of the positioning of the camera. Identifying and being conscious of this physical position should quickly reveal that we are also being invited to occupy a *social* space. A *social* space is also opened up for us by the text's mode of address, its setting, and its format. Finally, the physical and social spaces which we are invited to occupy are linked to *ideological* positions—"natural" ways of looking at and making sense of experience. (p. 229)

Masterman (1985) then gives an example of audience positioning in television news programs:

> As the news opens, we are addressed by a news reader who looks directly at the camera and delivers "the facts." Each viewer is given the role of direct addressee. We cut to a filmed interview. Our position changes. We are no longer directly addressed, but eavesdrop, watch and judge. The different positions assure us that some aspects of experience must be accepted (facts), whilst others (opinions) require our judgment. The highly questionable distinction within journalism between fact and opinion is sewn into the ways in which we are positioned in relation to different aspects of experience. (pp. 229–230)

What Masterman (1985) is suggesting is that in order to make sense of films or TV news *on their own terms*, the viewer must be able to adopt if only imaginatively and temporarily—the social, political, and economic interests that are the conditions for the knowledge they construct.

An educational film's address to the student, for example, invites her not only into the activity of knowledge construction but also into the construction of knowledge from a particular social and political point of view. This makes "viewing experience" and the sense that we make of films not simply voluntary and idiosyncratic, but relational—a projection of particular kinds of relations of self to self, and between self, others, knowledge, and power.

So, part of a 12-year-old boy's experience of and relationship to a film such as *Jurassic Park* is a response not only to its style and story. It is also a response to the ways in which its structure of address solicits, demands, even, a certain reading from him. His experience of the film includes the conscious and unconscious one of being addressed—through, for example, camera positioning and the social space it constructs "for" him—as if he were who the film wants him to be, thinks he is, or both.

"Who, Me?"

However, he never is exactly who the film thinks he is—12 years old, an American, white, suburban boy. None of these things ever means just one thing. None of these social positions is ever a single or unified one. Maybe he's a gay 12-year-old boy. What does that do to the usual assumptions about his 12-year-oldness, his whiteness, his suburbanness, his boyness? Maybe he's a mixed-race boy who is often "mistaken" for "white." Maybe he's 12 years old and the son of an abusive parent and has never really experienced being 12 years old. Maybe he lives in the suburbs but wishes he lived in the city and goes there every chance he gets.

The viewer is *never* only or fully who the film thinks s/he is. (The viewer is never exactly who *s/he* thinks s/he is either, but we'll save that one for later.) Depending on how far off the mark the film is about who we think we are, the experience of a film's mode of address ranges from "meeting/missing" the film from two seats to the left of the ideal seat in the theater, to meeting/missing it from the front row last seat against the wall. Both off-center seats require some reworking on the part of the viewer to bring the film into focus—some rewriting, reviewing, in order to get it from off center by imagining oneself to be at its center of address. Watching a film from frontrow last seat against the side wall solicits constant perceptual translation of the image—prompts the viewer to project herself into that perfect seat in the center of the theater and imagine how much better and more pleasing it must look from the place she "should" be sitting in.

So, too, being slightly or hugely missed by a film's mode of address requires what some film scholars have called "negotiation" on the part of the viewer. What does being 12 years old and a girl mean for getting pleasure from the story of *Jurassic Park*? But this negotiation is never a simple or a single thing either. Because just as the viewer is never exactly who the film thinks s/he is, the film is never exactly what *it* thinks it is. There's never just one unified mode of address in a film.

If *Jurassic Park* had been addressed strictly and solely to 12-year-old white American suburban boys, the rest of the planet would have been less likely than it was to go to see it. There was something in that film that was intended for who the filmmakers imagined me to be. (My guess is that the strong, brave, intelligent woman scientist was pitched to a part of me—even if it felt like she was put in grudgingly, and as an afterthought. And even if she was a much watered-down version of the woman scientist in *Jurassic Park*, the book.) So my negotiation of *Jurassic Park*'s modes of address was not simply a matter of having to imagine myself as a 12-year-old boy in order to get the film and enjoy it.

Multiple entry points into films is a commercial necessity. This complicates the whole notion of mode of address.

Angela McRobbie (1984) points this out in her study of how teenage girls responded to watching *Flashdance* and *Fame*. According to McRobbie, in both films, the dance scenes seem to be addressed primarily to two groups of heterosexual male spectators: those within the films' stories and those who watched the films in the theater. The musical numbers seem organized (through camera angles and placement, shot-reverse-shot editing) to appeal to the desires and visual pleasures that such an audience supposedly gets from watching women dance for them.

Yet, there are aspects of the stories of both of these films that are addressed primarily to women in the audience and to what the filmmakers consciously and unconsciously imagine to be women's desire for control over their bodies and for feeling pleasure and power in their bodies and lives. So a tension is set up *within* the modes of address of these films—a tension between who the dance numbers think you are and who the story thinks you are.

Both films' *stories* then complicate the issue of who the women are dancing "for" in the *spectacles* of the films' musical numbers. Teenage girls' pleasures in watching these films may come from reading the dancers as "really" dancing for themselves, not for the men who nevertheless are watching. Or, more complexly, teenage girls' pleasures may come from reading the dancers as "really" dancing for *both* themselves and the men watching them. The mode of address of the spectacle of the dance performances rubs up against the mode of address of the unfolding story line, and these two modes of address don't necessarily work together compatibly. Different formal and stylistic systems in a single film can have different modes of address. Multiple modes of address can be going on simultaneously.

Furthermore, once real live audiences come into the theater, a film's mode of address becomes just one among the many that make up a viewer's day. The position that a viewer "takes up" in relation to a film, and from which she makes sense of it and gets pleasure from it, shifts drastically depending on surrounding and competing modes of address. Is she watching a video of *Flashdance* with a group of girlfriends on a sleep over, in a theater with a boyfriend on a date, with her lesbian lover, as a student in a film class, as an African-American woman who rarely sees other African-American women on the big screen?

Mode of address in film, then, is about the necessity of addressing any communication, text, action, "to" someone. And, given the commercial interests of filmmakers, it is about the desire to control, as much as possible, how and from where the viewer reads the film. It's about enticing a viewer into a particular position of knowledge toward the text, a position of coherence from which the film works, makes sense, gives pleasure, satisfies dramatically and aesthetically, sells itself and its spin-off products.

But, as film scholars have tried to match up the mechanisms of address in a particular film's text with the readings that an actual audience has made of that film, they have had to become more and more attentive to the complications and paradoxes of the filmgoing experience. Audiences are not simply "placed" by a mode of address. Yet, to make any sense of a film or to enjoy it even minimally, they must engage with its mode of address. However minimally or obliquely, a film's mode of address is implicated in audiences' pleasures and interpretations—even in their refusals to go see a film at all.

"Yes, You."

This is where power relations and social change come in. Mode of address is not a neutral concept in film analysis. It's a concept that comes out of an approach to film studies that is interested in how filmmaking and film viewing get caught up in larger social dynamics and power relations.

While audiences can't simply be placed by a mode of address, modes of address do offer seductive encouragements and rewards for assuming those positions within gender, social status, race, nationality, attitude, taste, style, to which a film is addressed. No one in the global audience for *Jurassic Park* is its imagined and desired 12-year-old white American suburban boy. Yet, that subject position, however much it is mythical as a norm, is linked in the film to powerful fantasies of potency, prerogative, and control.

Most film scholars have liked some of the subject positions offered in popular films, and they haven't liked others. Those working from, for example, Marxist or feminist or humanist perspectives have used the concept of mode of address to "prove" that most popular films repeatedly offer a narrow and systematically biased range of subject positions. This narrow range excludes all sorts of other social and cultural perspectives and experiences. (Where are all the coming-of-age or adventure films addressed to 12-year-old girls—of any racial or ethnic background? Why does it seem right to place this question within parentheses?)

But the sins of mainstream Hollywood films are not just sins of omission. They are also sins of repeatedly implying, through exclusion, or through narrative ridicule or punishment, that being a girl (or being black or Asian or gay or fat or Spanish speaking or being a girl *and* one or other of these) is not the thing to be. Or, being a particular kind of girl or boy or Latino/and or fat kid may be OK, but being another kind is not OK.

To ask the question, Who does this film think you are, or want you to be? then, is to pose a loaded question. It's a question formulated by film scholars who think that who particular films think you are or want you to be may contribute to unequal power relations and the unconscious formation of individuals in society. And there are some individuals—masculinist sexist men and women, racists of any color, exploitative rich and powerful people, for example—and power dynamics that some film scholars don't want to see "formed" or rewarded by films' narratives and image systems.

"Not Me!"

Some filmmakers who are convinced that social and power relations may be affected by making and viewing films have launched experiments in various kinds of "counter cinema." Some feminist filmmakers, for example, have turned Hollywood conventions against themselves. They try to both call attention to and deny pleasures of film viewing that have relied on objectifying women's bodies and repressing women's agency.

Chantal Akerman, for example, in a 3½-hour-long narrative film that she made in 1975 titled *Jeanne Dielman*, documented three days in the life of a Belgian woman, a petit bourgeois widow, housewife, and mother. This is how Annette Kuhn (1982) describes the film:

> Her movements around her flat, her performance of everyday chores, are documented with great precision: many of her tasks are filmed in real time. Jeanne's rigid routine includes a daily visit from a man—a different one each day—whose fees for her sexual services help maintain her and her son. ...
>
> Domestic labor has probably never been documented in such painstaking detail in a fiction film; for example, one sequence-shot about five minutes in length shows Jeanne preparing a meat loaf for dinner on the third day ... the refusal of reverse shots in the film entails a denial of the "binding-in" effect of the suture of classic cinema: the spectator is forced to maintain a distance in relation to both narrative and image, constructing the story and building up narrative expectations for herself. (pp. 173–174)

The idea is that a film like *Jeanne Dielman* is more "open" and less manipulative in its positioning of its audience than is a Doris Day film about being a housewife. It refuses to use typical Hollywood modes of address that "bind" the spectator into one way of interpreting the film.

For example, Akerman refuses to take shots from Dielman's optical point of view. She refuses to use this convention of camera work familiar to audiences and often intended to rouse their empathy for and imaginative collusion with a character's intentions, experiences, goals. Being supposedly more open and less manipulative, *Jeanne Dielman*'s mode of address theoretically "empowers" the spectator to construct the story and build up narrative expectations for herself.

Experiments in counter cinemas have produced a whole host of strategies for addressing the audiences that are seldom or never seen in Hollywood films (such as the 5-minute-long static shot of Dielman making meat loaf). Such experiments have expanded the narrative and visual lexicon—and audience expectations—available to filmmakers. And, in some cases, these innovations have changed the politics of representation that reign in Hollywood (or, such innovations have been co-opted, depending on your allegiances).

The revolutionary hope was that changing modes of address in films might change the kinds of subject positions that are available and valued in society. Films like *Jeanne Dielman* might even produce new subjects of society—new kinds of "women," for example, empowered women who construct their own stories and expectations. Such films might, in other words, produce social change for the better.

But, this hasn't turned out to be a simple or direct matter, either. Films like *Jeanne Dielman* are hard to read when you're so used to reading Hollywood films. And when hard-to-read films that deny the usual and expected (sexist, racist, escapist) fantasies and pleasures become part of an intentional political strategy, well, as one film critic put it:

> The line between estrangement as a kind of passionate and thinking detachment and estrangement as alienation in the worst sense is obviously thin. (Cook, 1985, p. 220)

In other words, some films produced in the name of counter cinema and the empowerment of spectators were difficult to read or were alienating because of how they denied and negated conventional film viewing pleasures. Even worse, some of their intended audience didn't necessarily want to give up their guilty pleasures. Pleasure and fantasy may be political, but that's not all they are.

"Yes, Me (1), and Me (2), and Me (3), and ..."

Judith Mayne (1993) is a feminist film scholar. She's the kind of woman viewer to whom, it might be said, many of the feminist experiments in counter cinema were addressed. She writes:

> I may be an informed spectator, but that has not lessened my pleasure in what some consider inferior products, like Arnold Schwarzenegger films. Rather,

the study of spectatorship has made me cognizant, in quite commonplace and everyday ways, of the kinds of contradictory impulses that comprise pleasure. For as much as feminism, for instance, is fully part of my everyday life, I have somewhat peculiar (peculiar, that is, to my friends and family; not to me) regressive fantasies about male adolescence which are given perfect expression by Schwarzenegger. Spectatorship is one of the few places in my life where the attractions to male adolescence and feminist avant-garde poetics exist side by side. For Chantal Akerman's particular approach to spectatorship, for instance, engages me in different but equally satisfying ways as Arnold Schwarzenegger's. (p. 3)

As a filmgoer, Mayne is not only capable of acting against what her feminist friends and she herself would probably call her "best interests" "as a woman" in a male-dominated culture. She's also capable of desiring and enjoying such acting out even as she's doing it.

Now, that poses a big problem for people who think that mode of address can make the difference between spectatorship that is "critical," reflective, and passionately detached; and spectatorship that, as Mayne (1993) puts it, "makes me act out and forget" (p. 3) and actually collude in dominant and unjust cinematic and cultural practices, pleasures, and desires. Obviously, a film's mode of address isn't all-powerful.

Some film scholars have taken up the emphasis on reading in reader-response theory, and shifted the power in meaning-making to the viewer. They have conducted audience studies to try to understand and recognize the agency that viewers have always exercised at the movies. No matter how much the film's mode of address tries to construct a fixed and coherent position within knowledge, gender, race, sexuality, from which the film "should" be read; actual viewers have always read films against their modes of address, and "answered" films from places different from the ones that the film speaks to.

This shift in focus from the text's mode of address to the viewer's response to it has raised the issue of different readings not only within the same spectator—such as in Mayne's adolescent boy and feminist readings. It also raises the issue of different readings between different "kinds" of audiences.

Mayne and other film theorists have used black spectatorship and gay spectatorship as examples of places of film viewing that supposedly differ drastically from those addressed by mainstream cinema. How do audiences that are "black," "gay," or both, for example, read films never addressed to them?

Mayne (1993), for example, looks at this issue through James Baldwin's description of resistant black spectatorship of the film *The Defiant Ones* (1958). That film

> tells the tale of two escaped prisoners, one white (Tony Curtis) and one black ([Sidney] Poitier). During most of the film they are handcuffed to each other and through their relationship a parable of race relations in North America is told. (p. 155)

Because the film is a white myth of black and white relations, it

> contains numerous "blind spots" (to use the language of 1970s film theory) wherein Poitier's character acts, not as a black man, but as a white image of what a black man is. (p. 155)

The "truth" of Poitier's "blackness" was placed, in this film, at the mercy of the "lie" of the narrative's myth of black-white relations, its inability to "get it right." Yet, the truth of his blackness also foils the power of the narrative to completely have its way with Poitier's performance and the black audience's experience of it. To show that this is so, Mayne quotes James Baldwin's (1976/1990) description of "liberal white viewers" as cheering when Poitier jumped off the train at the conclusion of the film, "sacrificing his own chance to escape to remain with his white buddy" (p. 156). The "black Harlem audience" that Baldwin describes was, however, "outraged," yelling: *Get back on the train, you fool!*" (Baldwin, 1976/1990, p. 76).

"Who Do You Mean … 'We'?"

So film theorists recognize that all audiences are not the same, and that different audiences make different readings and get different, often opposing, pleasures from the same film. But this recognition has produced its own problems. For one, an unspoken assumption of much film theory is that if the targeted social position of Hollywood movie-making "is assumed to possess the attributes of 'dominance'—white, male, heterosexual, middle-class, etc." and Hollywood addresses itself to that position, then "'dominant' spectators [like the liberal white audience of *The Defiant Ones*] melt symbiotically into the screen" (Mayne, 1993, p. 159). "Dominant" spectators are assumed to "naturally" and unproblematically step into the position within the ideology and pleasure offered to them.

All "others" (like the black Harlem audiences) are considered marginal and resistant. And because resistance is not only interesting but also necessary to most political projects in film theory, audience studies have tended to focus on the so-called marginal and subcultural spectators. Typical research questions include the following: Do resistance and difference exist in the face of Hollywood's seductive and homogenizing address? Where? Who resists? Who is different? How do they resist and maintain difference? How can we cause difference and resistance to spread?

The problem with this approach, Mayne (1993) argues, is that it sets up a "dualism of 'dominant' spectators versus 'marginal' (and therefore resisting ones)," and it "perpetuates the false dichotomy of us and them" even as it tries to alleviate it. "Defining the other as the vanguard of spectatorship only reverses the dichotomy" (p. 159).

Further, it's still not clear to those working in the field of film studies just "what" an "audience" "is." Using notions of identity and identity politics to study what various social groups supposedly do with films hasn't made things much clearer. To speak of a gay audience, for example, suggests that "all gay men and lesbians share some specific identification patterns ... or some kind of inherent capacity to read against the grain" (Mayne, 1993, p. 166). But it's just as impossible to identify a common experience of gay male or lesbian viewing (not to mention, therefore, gay and lesbian) as it is to identify a single mode of spectatorship for blacks, women, or 12-year-old white boys. In fact, literary critics and film scholars are not arguing that there are strong homosexual currents in *all* reading and film spectatorship, and that an African-American presence informs *all* U.S. cultural texts in ways that shape white readers' experiences of themselves and others (Sedgwick, 1990; Morrison, 1992). So much for the usually applied distinctions between center and margin.

Still, Mayne (1993) argues, academic writing about the "politics" of critical spectatorship usually remains locked into an either/or scenario. Either we're talking of a micropolitics of the viewer or the marginal social group, where every reading is a contestatory act because the film's mode of address never fits perfectly. Or, because such localized, subcultural acts of resistant reading supposedly don't add up to social change, we're talking a "macropolitics where nothing is contestatory unless part of a globally defined political agenda" (p. 172).

As in all academic endeavors, political interests drive theories of how people view films, and how they *should* view films. As Mayne (1993) puts it, "the very purpose of academic spectatorship studies was to encourage the development of critical spectatorship, certainly to the extent that the large majority of those who write film scholarship also teach" (p. 165). By "critical," Mayne does not mean merely educated or informed spectatorship. She means spectatorship that actively resists colluding with mainstream films in producing meanings that simply reinscribe the objectification of women's bodies and lives, heterosexist "normality," economic exploitation, and racist stereotypes, for example.

Many of the people studying and teaching films have wanted to better understand how audiences read films so that audiences can be better taught how to read films resistantly. Underlying these studies is the desire, as Foucault (1979) might have put it, to discipline and stylize viewers' (students') uncritical readings into critical readings.

But most of us who are interested in fostering social change suffer lapses in critical spectatorship—like those of Mayne's indulgences in adolescent boy fantasies via Schwarzenegger films. And these (pleasurable, partially welcomed) lapses point to some of the dilemmas that dog most theories of social change and trouble the political and education strategies launched in their names.

Mode of Address as Event

In the absence of predictable and controllable "fits" between modes of address and spectator experience, some film theorists have stopped trying to pin a "kind" of resistant spectatorship to each kind of (marginalized) audience as it responds to various kinds of modes of address. They have shifted their attention from mode of address as a relatively static aspect of a film's text to mode of address as a more fluid aspect of the contexts in which viewers *use* films. Mayne (1993) describes this shift in emphasis as one away from questions such as, How do gay and lesbian audiences resist mainstream films' modes of address; and towards questions such as, What part does film watching play in how people and groups imagine and constitute various social and cultural identities and cultures? How do modes of address themselves get taken up and used, along with a wide-ranging web of texts and contexts, including rumor and gossip, in the construction of identities, cultural practices, and organized, politicized groups? How does camp, for example—which could be understood as an exaggeration of the ways that modes of address miss everyone—work as a shared social pleasure within gay and lesbian communities? How does film viewing get used in constituting lesbians and gays as a political force—such as when gays organize as a consumer group to challenge homophobic representation in films (p. 166)?

Mode of Address—Unresolved Issues

By asking, Who does this film think you are? Film scholars have come up with some pretty interesting ideas and arguments about the workings of narrative structures and visual systems in actual films. It's hard, for example, to disagree with the claim that films speak from somewhere within currently circulating ideas, fantasies, anxieties, desires, hopes, events—that "somewhere" can be located by looking at the ways certain characters, voices, points of view, discourses, and actions are visually and narratively privileged and rewarded over others in the film.

It's also hard to disagree with the claim that such privileging and rewarding through mode of address is an attempt by filmmakers to anticipate and speak to a desired audience's anxieties, fears, tastes, hopes, and ways of making sense. It seems clear that by speaking to these, a film tries to meet its imagined and desired audience at the place of its fears and hopes. Even if the audience is never in the place that the film speaks to, the place that the film addresses does seem to exist as an abstract and shareable "there," an imagined subject position within power, knowledge, and desire that the conscious and unconscious interests behind the making of the film "need" audiences to fill. Abstractly or not, films seem to "invite" actual viewers into such positions and "encourage" them to at least imaginatively assume and read the film from there. And viewers appear to be "rewarded" (with narrative pleasure, with happy endings, with coherent reading experiences) for "taking up" and acting from that imagined position as they interpret the film.

Yet, most film theorists would agree that questions about the relationship between the abstract position supposedly assigned to the film's viewers by its mode of address and the actual person who watches a movie, have not been resolved. Our pleasures in the movies stubbornly refuse any rigid dichotomies between simple, pure acts of highly receptive, complicit reproduction of the positions offered us on the one hand, and critical resistance to or refusal of those positions on the other.

What does seem clear to me after 25 years of film studies is that the relationships between how film texts address their audience, and how actual film spectators read films, are not neat or tidy—nor are they linear or causal. And the search for neat and tidy, linear and causal relationships is not an innocent one. As Mayne (1993) puts it, the kinds of questions about mode of address that film researchers have framed have been "haunted" questions. They are questions haunted by desires to fulfill "the possibility of spectatorship as a potential vanguard activity" for progressive political agendas (p. 172). Such desires are driven by a totalizing politics: Your interpretations of film are either resistant and therefore revolutionary or complicit and therefore reactionary. Film studies are now grappling with the meanings of the postmodern stance that a totalizing politics—even if it's intended to be progressive—is not attainable, and perhaps, ultimately, not desirable.

Film studies still have not got convincing answers to the questions, What difference does a film's mode of address make? Does the mode of address make a difference to who the viewer consciously and unconsciously thinks s/he is? What difference does who a viewer thinks s/he is make to how s/he acts in the world? Can different/other modes of address provoke or encourage different/other ways of being and acting in the world?

Can social change, in other words, start from or be fueled by the ways in which audiences are addressed by films, or both?

And because all education is about change, as an educator I rewrite some of these questions: Can social change or individual changes in the ways someone understands the world start from and be fueled by the ways students are addressed by curriculum and pedagogy?

Can—do—teachers make a difference in power, knowledge, and desire, not only by *what* they teach but also by *how* they *address* students?

These are unresolved questions in film studies. And they are questions unasked in education.

References

Baldwin, J. (1963; rpt. 1988). A Talk to Teachers. In R. Simonson & S. Walker (Eds.), *Multi-Cultural Literacy* (pp. 3–12). Saint Paul, MN: Graywolf Press.

Baldwin, J. (1976; rpt. 1990). The Devil Finds Work. New York: Dell.

Cook, P. (ed.). (1985). *The Cinema Book: A Complete Guide to Understanding the Movies.* New York: Pantheon Books.

Donald, J. (ed.). (1991). *Psychoanalysis and Cultural Theory: Thresholds.* London: Macmillan Education.

Foucault, M. (1979). *Discipline and Punish: The Birth of the Prison.* New York: Vintage Books.

Kuhn, A. (1982). *Women's Pictures: Feminism and Cinema.* London: Routledge & Kegan Paul.

Masterman, L. (1985). *Teaching the Media.* London: Comedia.

Mayne, J. (1993). *Cinema and Spectatorship.* New York: Routledge.

McRobbie, A. (1984). Dance and Social Fantasy. In A. McRobbie & M. Nava (Eds.), *Gender and Generation* (pp. 130–161). London: Macmillan.

Morrison, T. (1992). *Playing in the Dark: Whiteness and the Literary Imagination.* Cambridge, MA: Harvard University Press.

Sedgwick, E. K. (1990). *Epistemology of the Closet.* Berkeley, CA: University of California Press.

Chapter Four

Altered States of Vision: Film, Video, and the Teaching of Architectural History

BARRY BERGDOLL

The academic discipline of art history came of age with the slide projector at the end of the nineteenth century and, as any college graduate knows, has been married to it ever since. The alliance of photography with the technology of the magic lantern in the 1850s made it possible to transform any darkened room into a museum or a site visit to the Nile Valley, the Athenian Acropolis, or the Roman Forum. And with the growth of commercial lantern slide companies, even the most remote university and art or architecture school could possess a private museum of reproductions for classroom teaching.[1] With the introduction of commercial color slides in the 1940s, the last practical obstacle to teaching the history of painting with substitutes for originals was removed. Aside from laments that slides cannot capture the texture or subtle range of hues of the original, and that all works in the history of art assume the same scale on the screen, the photographic representation in art history has increasingly been accepted as a reproduction, as viable for contemporary instruction as the plaster casts and oil copies were in the art schools of previous centuries. Courses in art appreciation might still insist on the original as the unique object of study. But only the slide collection has been able to realize André Malraux's dream of a *musée imaginaire*,[2] in which the juxtaposition of works of art from the most remote locations, and of the extant with the destroyed, grants anyone a visual command of the entire history of art. Donald Preziosi goes so far as to claim, in his provocative critique *Rethinking Art History*, that "the modern discipline of art history presupposes the existence of photography from its beginnings," and that "filmic technologies have played a key role in analytic study, taxonomic ordering, and the creation of historical and genealogical narratives."[3]

Photography and Architectural History

Architectural history has had a somewhat different relation to photography, at once more precocious and more resistant. For although architectural photography achieved a higher degree of accuracy much earlier than the photographic reproduction of paintings, architecture was not so easily moved into the classroom.[4] An art historian can discuss a work of art at length with a single slide; however, a building can only be presented with a whole battery of images. The very minimum required to reconstruct, even in a fragmented way, the spatial and structural reality of a building or an urban space is a range of different views of the exterior and interior.

But even here it is helpful to have recourse to representations of another kind to lend coherency to these individual views, namely the orthographic projections that have, since the Renaissance, been the preferred way of conceiving and recording architectural designs: plan, section, and elevation.[5] These are not only vital for relating the photographic views to the totality of the building, but they also remind us that architectural history had a commerce with representations long before the photograph made it possible, as Viollet-le-Duc noted, to have "an exact and irrefutable presentation of a building in any given state," almost as though one could have the building in one's pocket for continual reference.[6]

Yet, while photographs and drawings might be juxtaposed on a slide screen to submit a building to analysis, the building itself remains obstinately absent from the classroom. In particular, the interlocked experiences of space and time vital to the discovery and comprehension of buildings *in situ* are impossible to re-create in projected still images. By careful orchestration, and with a multiplication of views, the sequence of movement through a building—the shifts in luminosity and scale; the changes in color and texture; the differing quality of interior spaces—might be evoked and something of the actual experience of moving through a building simulated. This densely packed and quickly paced slide sequence seems almost to recapitulate the birth of cinema itself from the rapid stringing together of still photographic images.

Is film then the technology that renders most transparent the reproduction of architecture in the space of the classroom? Can film finally overcome the dilemma of lectures and exhibitions on architecture, seeking always to reconstitute the totality of a work of architecture by the multiplication of individual representations, by turning its own simulation of the human eye to recording the visual reality of this still medium that can only be discovered by movement in time and space? Does film's ability to suppress our awareness of the individual frame allow it to supersede the slide as the best way of teaching architectural history off-site?

It is not only the capturing of architecture but the construction of history itself that seems to lend itself so effortlessly to the nature of cinematic representation of reality. For Preziosi, art history, whether consciously or not, "has been a supremely cinematic practice, concerned with the orchestration of historical narratives and the display of genealogy by filmic means. In short, the modern discipline has been grounded in metaphors of cinematic practice to the extent that in nearly all of its facets, art history could be said to continually refer to and implicate the discursive logic of realist cinema."[7]

Whether or not one is willing to accept this sweeping generalization, or its implicit critique of art historical practices, Preziosi provokes us to think about the way art historians themselves relate images to larger structures of explanation. Film then, with its possibility of simulating more convincingly than any other medium the presence of architecture, and its possibility of simulating the collage-like montage already inherent to the practice of much current academic architectural history, would seem predestined to a success in the classroom that might rival that of the almighty slide.

Historians' Resistance to Film

Why then have academic architectural historians been so resistant to trading in their slides for film and video that make it possible, at the flick of a switch, to convert the still image on the screen into a moving one? Without yielding further to Preziosi's invitation to deconstruct the ideological implications of art history, there are two entrenched forms of resistance to the use of film in teaching architectural history that must be evoked before turning to the main theme of this essay, which is the possibilities and limitations of using film and video for teaching architectural history. These return to the two terms of the discipline: architecture and history.

It is a commonplace that movement and time are the essence of both film and architecture and thus that the fit between the two is a natural one. Yet, anyone who has held a video camera up to a building can tick off the inherent difficulties of filming architecture, and anyone who knows and loves a building and has sat through a television documentary on it knows how infrequently a film actually leaves one with the sensation of knowing a building. The specific difficulties are perhaps too obvious to merit more than a rapid check list. Already the frame presents a problem. For although a still camera can be oriented to produce either a horizontal or vertical format image, the film or video screen is, by convention, a standardly proportioned horizontal rectangle. Towering cathedral façades and spires or soaring American skyscrapers, for instance, must be photographed from afar, with a distorting lens, or else submit to the vertical panning shots that are the standard stuff of most films on the skyscraper.

Here, one has nostalgia for some of the triumphs of architectural photography of the 1920s and 1930s, such as Berenice Abbott's unusual skinny vertical formats to capture the surge in height and the narrow canyons of Wall Street. Although the film camera can follow the footstep and the eye, and even both, it cannot capture the seamless relationship between vision and body that is part of the experience of architectural space. And whereas the experience of the building involves the selection of a path, voluntary or involuntary, a film provides a preselected route that not only levels the psychological cues of architectural space but also inevitably replaces our choices with those of the director.

The invisible director is in control of the syntax of representing space and of the tempo and rhythm of movement both on the shoot-tracking shot, pan, or the sinuous movement of the steadicam—and on the editing table. Space, the very essence of architecture, in the cinema is always represented or translated by a director and cameraman, rather than experienced directly. Knowledge, perception, and memory do not operate the same way in architectural space as they do in celluloid space.

The resistance to using films from the point of view of history is likewise one of an unwillingness to relinquish directorial control. For although the slide is a pictorial foil to a lesson, an argument, or a discourse developed by the historian in a classroom lecture, the film is a construct of its own, with its own "voice" in both images and sound track. Rather than being a handmaiden, the film might well be seen as a usurpation or competition with the historian's own voice. Relatively few existing films would win the wholesale approval of any specialist, either for content or visual approach, so that programming a series of films—although this has been tried with varying success by television channels and universities of the air[8]—requires either an abdication of the professorial lectern or a radical reinterpretation of it.

This essay is an exploration of the latter possibility, a possibility that is opened once the film's nature as a representation is acknowledged and embraced. Film and video indeed have the potencial to become, if not the new spouse of architectural history, at least one of the most potent forms of representation with which it has commerce in the analysis of its absent object.

The Technological Classroom

Imagine the ideal architectural history classroom of the future, with its multimedia wall controlled from the lecturer's podium. At the flick of a switch, students can move from the contemplation of still images—architectural drawings or photographs projected as slides—to the experience of moving images in film or video, and even to computer/video screens that allow the introduction of the most advanced computer analyses of spaces and the virtual reality re-creations of others—in short, a flat wall on which every representation of the third dimension could be projected, exploited, and juxtaposed. Immediately, many of the logistical obstacles of using film and video in the classroom are removed, from the clumsiness of shifting from one type of equipment to another, to the interruption of the dialogue between an instructor's narrative and a range of visual evidence being interrogated in front of the class. Remote control in hand, the instructor can move freely in the film, freeze a frame, reverse, select, and enter into dialogue with the film in a way common in film history classes (even if disrespectful to the integrity of the film as a work of cinematic art).

This animated wall might even help combat one of the great cultural problems of using film and video tapes in classrooms, namely that for those of us raised on television, the television screen more often than not induces a passivity profoundly at odds with the best learning. Moreover, current television standards can scarcely admit such standard pedagogical techniques as reiteration, prolonged investigation of a single image or concept, and continual realignment of ideas with new concepts and examples, which would imply a film composed largely of long fixed frames, slow camera movements, and repetition. On the other hand, many educational videos on architecture, where such pedagogical criteria are allowed to govern the filming and editing, are more often than not little more than "disguised" lectures; juxtaposing shots of the presenter, still photography, filmed sequences, and diagrams, they are often lacking in the spontaneity, interaction, or intuitive response to an audience that marks the success of the best teachers. The first is bad architectural viewing, the second bad teaching. So just how can the techniques and conventions of pedagogy and film be made to support rather than combat one another?

This future "media wall" reminds us that even the technological classroom will always be a site of multiple representations. Unless virtual reality should replace shelter itself, buildings will continue to exist as singular concrete moments in a chain of representations that runs from the architect's first conceptual sketches (and indeed their relationship to all the other images in the architect's mind or library of resources) to the images by which the completed building is publicized outside its local context via the professional press, architectural exhibitions, or the media of film and television.

As architectural history in the last generation or so has broadened its purview, abandoning the scenario of a repertoire of great buildings and their architects for the study of the practice of architecture in its cultural, political, and economic setting, the analysis of architectural representations *as representations* has become an integral part of the discipline's method. Imagine a course on Renaissance architecture, for instance, that glossed over the issue of the rise of perspective rendering and its implications for spatial design, or a course in nineteenth-century architecture that failed to address the rise of the architectural press and its impact on the circulation of images that made possible architectural eclecticism. Or imagine a course on early twentieth-century modernism that did not consider the crucial impact on architectural design of new photographic technologies, both increasingly less expensive still photographs and the new motion picture cameras. Or, for that matter, how could one teach a course on recent architecture that did not address the influence of cinematographic framing and notation on contemporary figures such as Rem Koolhaas or Bernard Tschumi in late twentieth-century culture, when the language and experience of film images pervade the way we experience and perceive the world?

Le Corbusier in the Media Classroom

Let's take for an example a class on Le Corbusier in the 1920s in this future media classroom. The lecturer will orchestrate the projection of a range of slides showing the development, final design, and construction of Le Corbusier's famous villas, before passing to actual views—both historical and contemporary—of the buildings. But certainly the analysis would not remain circumscribed by the documents directly involved in the creation of the object. Le Corbusier's various uses of photographic media in designing and publicizing his work would need to be analyzed.

And not only the famous photographic juxtapositions in such texts as *Towards a New Architecture* (1923) or his articles in the review *L'Esprit Nouveau*,[9] but also the films that Le Corbusier himself made at the Villa Stein at Garches in 1927 and at the Villa Savoye at Poissy in 1929 would be an integral part of describing the way Le Corbusier understood architecture as part of contemporary avant-garde culture. This not only completes the chain of representations from conception to publicity, but also provides an opportunity to engage the class in the discussion of the relationship between Le Corbusier's architecture and filmmaking. In Le Corbusier's case, the dialogue is particularly close since the architect imagined his villas developing along what he called "architectural promenades," which were at once re-creations of the ceremonial processional routes mapped out on sites that had affected him powerfully as he traveled through Italy, Greece, and the Near East, and sequences of frames that might well make up the story board of a modern film.

For instance, not only does the Villa Savoye seem to recapture in modern terms the sequence of views that Le Corbusier sketched, photographed, and arranged as a voyage recording his experience of the Athenian Acropolis, but the designed building also seems almost to script his future film on the villa. At the Villa Savoye, the entire circulation pattern is conceived as a journey that begins outside on the road, exploits a series of frames through the windshield of the car whose turning radius traces the sweep of the great curved wall of the ground floor, and culminates in the pedestrian rhythms of a long, gentle ramp that zigzags from ground to roof terrace and organizes all the internal spaces of the building. Here is a building in which the syntax of the space and the syntax of film seem almost two dialects of the same language. A classroom discussion of the language of Le Corbusier's film on the Villa Savoye of the early 1930s and the cinematographic philosophy and syntax of one of the several documentaries on Le Corbusier—for instance, the Open University production titled *Le Corbusier: Villa Savoye* (1975), or the three-part series, *Le Corbusier* (1987), by Jacques Barsac produced for French television in the year of the Le Corbusier centenary—would provide the opportunity both to engage students in a historical discussion of the relationship between early modernist architecture and 1920s cinema and to begin making the students aware of and articulate about the language of cinema itself.

Developing Visual Literacy

It seems to me that if films are to be incorporated into the architectural history curriculum as more than either a simulated visit or a filmed lecture, students must be taught to read the conventional language of film just as they are now taught to read the conventional language of graphic representations of architecture. What instructor in architectural history does not make certain early on that the students know how to decipher the standard codes and conventions of floor plans, sections, and elevations? In my undergraduate courses at Columbia University, I require the students in introductory courses to draw these three projections—plan, section, and elevation—of a familiar space on campus, usually McKim, Mead, and White's Low Library, to familiarize them with the most common representations used in architectural history and to begin to internalize their notational relation to real built space.

One of the most gratifying moments for me in teaching a course a few years ago at Columbia's semester-abroad program in Paris was a session where the students viewed the first part of Jacques Barsac's *Le Corbusier* in which archival footage, archival stills, and new filmed footage are brilliantly integrated with a sound track composed principally of Le Corbusier's own voice from historic recordings. The film culminates in a visit to the Villa Savoye. The students had visited the villa several weeks earlier and had been asked to draw a ground plan of the first two floors while we were on the site. Later they listened to a classroom lecture on the building. Barsac was able to come to the next class when the students viewed his film and to take questions and lead a discussion on his ambitious project. The students asked questions, pointed as well as appreciative, about the way he had filmed the building. They wondered, for instance, why he had started with an elevated point of view rather than on the ground, although they agreed that his tracking shots captured beautifully the path that Le Corbusier almost imposes on the visitor through the seemingly open space of his free plan.

The pump admittedly had been well primed, for the students were enrolled simultaneously in my courses on modern French architecture and urbanism and in a course with French filmmaker Nadine Descendre on the city and the cinema, involving not only the history of

Paris but also the history of its representations in film and cinema. The final project in that course was to make a film that could be used in my courses, and the entire class of art history majors wrote and directed a four-minute film on the Odeon Theater and its place in the theatrical urbanism of its eighteenth-century Paris quarter. Here, instead of making an argument by translating the visual and spatial language of building into the words of the traditional essay or term paper, the students were required to translate one visual language into another.

Short of requiring students to take courses in architectural design, this project tested the ways in which the language of cinema can be used to enhance students' awareness of the ways in which architects structure space and experience. The film project obliged the students to analyze a space and its structure with a care and depth that few other assignments could stimulate. In addition, it reinforced a central aspect of historical method in architectural history: learning to derive evidence from form rather than always seeking reinforcement or ultimate answers in textual sources. Thus again, both for sharpening a student's eye and for honing a sense of the method of historical inquiry in architectural history, film can be used innovatively in fruitful ways.

Of course, few university courses in architectural history have the luxury of time or financial means or the freedom of interdisciplinary teaching that was possible in that experimental setting; however, my example illustrates the point that consciously addressing the nature of filmmaking, making the awareness of its limitations and possibilities for representing architecture part of the curriculum itself, converts the film from a passive simulation of visiting a building into a powerful tool for involving students in the analysis of architecture.

Computer Simulations of Architecture

The example of Barsac's film on Le Corbusier introduces another powerful tool that video has made available not only to architectural teaching but also to history itself—the computer simulation of unbuilt or destroyed spaces. In an extraordinary sequence, Barsac seamlessly integrates actual footage of contemporary Paris with a computer simulation of Le Corbusier's Plan Voisin (1925), the famous and controversial proposal to replace a large portion of central Paris with a district of high-rise office towers and ranges of housing in park-like settings. Never before has either professional or layman had such a vivid representation of Le Corbusier's unrealized urban utopia, and never before has anyone—perhaps not even Le Corbusier—been in a position to judge so directly the projected appearance and impact of his ideas on the city. Barsac's use of the recently developed techniques linking computer-generated images and video to explore a proposal of the 1920s might be disputed by historical purists, but even more than a three-dimensional wooden or plaster model, the video simulation achieves a presence that transforms both the student's understanding and that of the specialist who discovers this well-known proposal in a wholly new light. I have found in using Le Corbusier sequences from Barsac's films that my seminars on modernist urbanism take on an incredible intensity in which each student is engaged.

Arguably, the teaching of urban form, even more than architecture, benefits tremendously from the use of film. Barsac's film becomes all the more powerful and provocative if juxtaposed with a film that sets out to capture the essence of Haussmann's Paris, the very tradition that Le Corbusier's urbanism challenges. The most poetic and successful of these to my mind is *Paris—Story of a City* (1991), a brilliant realization of the visual arguments of François Loyer's revisionist reading of the urban form of Paris.[10] In an era in which architectural design itself is embracing the latest technologies in co mputer graphics, and simulation and video technology are being combined with the construction of both real three-dimensional and simulated computer models to allow architects and community groups to discuss the impact of various alternatives in architectural and urban designs,[11] it seems only inevitable that architectural history expand the range of its representations without waiting for these new representations to become part of the repertoire of its archival documents.

The Wedding of Film Technique and Architecture

Certain types of films lend themselves more fruitfully to teaching than others, and not coincidentally they tend to be films that have set out in their very approach to an architectural subject to achieve something at once specific to film or video but which takes its inspiration from the nature or structure of the work of architecture being interrogated by the camera and the film's voices. Admittedly, many films are of interest simply on an archival or documentary level: they present an interview with an architect (for instance, filmed interviews with Frank Lloyd Wright), or they contain footage of a demolished building, or they record the design, construction, or restoration process of an important building. Such films will inevitably be shown in their own right by a historian, but it is films that seek a specific fit between film technique and the subject that tend to be the most successful, not only as film art but also as teaching tools.

As a participant in the expermental Production Laboratory 12 in the late 1980s, in which for a number of years in the late 1980s and early 1990s the Program for Art on Film, a joint venture of the Getty Foundation and of the Metropolitan Museum of Art, set out to investigate the qualities that make a good documentary by fostering collabrions bweeen filmmakers and art and architectural historians, I was sturck by the interest shared by the overwhelming number of teams in exploring the ways we look at works of art.

Several films in the series took particularly innovative approaches, some with origins in feature film making but novel in their application to documetnary film making. For instance, Takahiko Iimura and Arata Isozaki's film *Ma: Space/time in the Garden of Ryoan-Ji* (1989) presents no historical information about the famous Zen garden in Kyoto, but provides a powerful visual commentary on the intentions and experiences of looking at such a garden. One after another, tracking shots of the garden are introduced with variant itineraries, various rhythms of close-ups and long shots, and various durations; each one is accompanied by a thought about the garden, almost a haiku, and gradually the film powerfully conveys the idea that the garden exists not as an iconographic construct but as a stimulus to the imagination in which space and time, the essence of the architecture experience, are interrelated. The film itself then becomes an experience of *"ma,"* which the authors feel is an inherently Japanese concept.

Although many might dispute filmmaker Takahiko Iimura's specific camera angles or pans, and others might take issue with the thesis of architect Arata Isozaki concerning the long tradition of Japanese interest in *"ma"* or the simultaneity and dependency of space and time, the film is self-consciously about how we see and experience this garden, conveying both the act and the spirit of contemplation of the Zen work of art that no projected slide or still image could possibly convey. Even its refusal of film conventions common in the West imposes a different rhythm of looking and seeing that comes as a revelation to a Western audience.

Another production in the series, Edin Velez and Jerrilynn Dodds's *A Mosque in Time* (1990), exploits the capacity of overlays and synthesized imagery in video to play with a very different notion of the experience of time in space by encouraging us to see in the surfaces of the Great Mosque at Córdoba (now a cathedral) the overlays and simultaneity of cultures in Andalusian Spain. Whether the viewer returns to a textbook on Spanish architectural history or a tour of the Mozarabic architecture of Spain itself, the building will never be seen in precisely the same way again.

It seems to me that film and video, more powerfully than any of the numerous forms of reproduction by which we can know, study, and discuss architecture, landscape, and urban space, can offer us such suggestive and at times provocative ways of seeing and looking that we return to the monuments of architectural history themselves with a different eye. In experimental films such as these, as well as in many of the most successful films catalogued by the Art on Film Database project, such invitations to alternative ways of viewing demonstrate how modes of viewing and seeing are themselves culturally and historically determined. This, when it can be conveyed to a student as more than a received idea, is an immeasurable gain for architectural history.

Notes

1. Thomas Sandby, the first professor of architecture at the Royal Academy in London, began giving lectures with reproductions of architectural monuments in 1770. There is some evidence that in addition to the large-scale drawings used by some of his successors, notably Sir John Soane, Sandby had drawings made on glass slides for projection. The earliest commercialized slides aimed at art historical instruction seem to have been in the 1880s, to judge by some trade

publications, such as Bruno Meyer, *Glasphotogramme fur den Kunstwissenschaftliche Unterricht* (Karlsruhe: The Author, 1883). Allan Harquard lectured with slides at Princeton from 1882, but it was not until the 1890s that the widespread availability of slides transformed art historical instruction and publications blossomed. See Howard B. Leighton, "The Lantern Slide and Art History," *History of Photography* 8 (1984): 107–118. See also Elizabeth Shephard, "The Magic Lantern Slide in Entertainment and Education, 1860–1920," *History of Photography* 11 (1987): 91–108.

2. André Malraux, *Le musée imaginaire* (Paris, 1947; 2nd edition 1965); taken up as the first section of his more widely known and read *Les Voix du Silence* (Paris, 1951). The term is usually translated as a *museum without walls*, which misses the dual sense of the French "imaginaire," meaning both *of images* and *of the imagination*.

3. Donald Preziosi, *Rethinking Art History: Meditations on a Coy Science* (New Haven: Yale University Press, 1989), p. 72.

4. For obvious reasons, exterior views of buildings were preferred subjects of early photographers; see Richard Pare and Phyllis Lambert, *Photography and Architecture, 1839–1939* (Montreal: Canadian Centre for Architecture, 1982), and Cervin Robinson and Joel Herschman, *Architecture Transformed: A History of the Photography of Buildings from 1839 to the Present* (New York: The Architectural League of New York, 1987).

5. For issues of architectural representation, see most recently Eve Blau and Edward Kaufman, *Architecture and Its Image: Four Centuries of Architectural Representation* (Montreal: Canadian Centre for Architecture, 1989).

6. Viollet-Ie-Duc, "Restoration" in *Dictionnaire raisonné de l'architecture* (Paris, 1866), vol. 8, p. 33; here quoted from the translation by Kenneth Whitehead in B. Bergdoll (ed.), *Viollet-le-Duc: The Foundations of Architecture* (New York: Braziller, 1990), p. 225.

7. Preziosi, *Rethinking Art History*, pp. 72–73.

8. The two best known recent American endeavors have been Robert A.M. Stern's *Pride of Place* and Spiro Kostof's *America by Design*, radically different series devoted to the history of American architecture, now available on videocassette. The Open University in England has been producing television series since the 1960s, but these are intended not as independent films but as part of a curriculum with supporting textbooks, viewing guides, and written essays and exams by correspondence.

9. On Le Corbusier's use of photographs, see Beatriz Colomina, "Le Corbusier and Photography," *Assemblage* 4 (1987), pp. 7–24.

10. Loyer's book, *Paris XIXe siècle: l'immeuble et la rue* (Paris: Hazan, 1987), has profoundly influenced recent interpretations of the meaning of the great transformation of Paris under the Second Empire (1852–1870).

11. For instance, the Environmental Simulation laboratories at the University of California, Berkeley, and at the New School for Social Research, New York.

12. This essay was originally written as one of a series of introductry texts to a catalogue of films, including primarily the films of the Metropolitan Museum of Art/Getty Foundation Program for Art on Film, and thus makes specific reference to the experimental works produced for that program, including my own film done in collaboration with French filmmaker Nadine Descendre, Sainte Genevieve: The Pantheon of Domes (1989). See also the conference report, Art History and Film (New York: Program for Art on Film, 1991).

Chapter Five

Human Rights Films Seeding Peace Education: Case Study Brazil

PETER LUCAS

Human Rights and Representation

Many scholars today believe that we have entered a new generation of human rights based on the emergence of transnational crimes against humanity. Although the 1990s was a brutal decade for collective violence around the world, it was also an amazing ten years for the growth of international human rights. This new generation is based on the emerging ability to prosecute gross violations transnationally, the explosive growth of international nongovernmental organizations (NGOs), the proliferation of human rights representation, and the flowering of human rights and peace education programs.

Representation is key in the study of human rights. Faced with serious violations, someone has to write up the details and convey the message to a larger audience. Today, human rights and representation has become a subfield of the larger movement involving journalists, researchers, and visual media workers. We have more books and reports about human rights than ever before. Photojournalists working from a humanist perspective are documenting suffering, injustice, and crimes against humanity. In many of the major cities of the world, there are now special human rights film festivals that include both documentary and feature films. And many visual artists now consider themselves as working in the classic human rights tradition of bearing witness. The exposure that representation brings to human rights today is so vital that it would be hard to conceive of the contemporary movement without visualizing the struggle in concrete forms.

For the past several years, I've been teaching a graduate course on human rights and representation, which introduces students to various representational strategies. The course covers many themes such as photojournalism, documentary films, media activism via the Internet, narrative strategies when writing about human rights, the use of theater to elicit human rights stories, the study of visual memorials after collective violence, and many other topical issues. The mix of students is impressive. No longer are law and political science students the only ones studying human rights. Most of my students are educators, future NGO workers, and media artists who envision themselves working with representation within the human rights movement.

Representation has multiple roles within the movement. First, representation is crucial in the identification process of locating a problematic situation that warrants a larger human rights dimension. This recognition is not a given. Mainstream media accounts of violence often fail to frame the issues in the broader context of international human rights standards. From a domestic vantage point, such as New York where I am writing from, human rights violations are usually seen as something that happens far away, involving street kids in Brazil or sexual slavery in Thailand. If people can read an article in the *New York Times* about homeless youth in Manhattan and not recognize the human rights issues at stake, then there's a serious problem of identification. I assume that this blind spot regarding the identification process plays out in many other locations as well. When teaching, I use domestic case studies as much as possible to highlight this very problem and to stress that human rights are as much about what happens close to home as what happens in distant places. This critical identification process is also about someone having the courage to call attention to a troubled spot in the world. What they locate is violence in its systemic nature and its various manifestations. Violence is the core problematic in human rights and peace education. But before it can be addressed and changed, it first has to be identified and made visible.

Beyond identification, representation also illuminates the universal human rights standards. The normative standards give us a moral philosophy to draw on, a discourse that helps us to converse and make sense of a given situation, and a legal set of barometers for redress. The many standards that now exist beyond the Universal Declaration of Human Rights are the scaffolding underneath the wider movement and guide us when responding to specific cases. The standards are also the main conceptual frameworks with which to study human rights. As conceptual frameworks, the standards work as a set of core organizing ideas that emphasizes the process of understanding the value of rights and the interrelationships between all standards in a holistic way. As important as the standards are, they can remain "paper rights" or one-dimensional without concrete forms of representation. It's always representation and the tradition of narrative that brings the themes of human rights to life.

Representation of human rights violations often triggers a response. People respond in social movements and civil society as advocates, activists, and as professional human rights workers for NGOs. To be sure, the possible responses for any given situation are many, which may or may not include representation. Many NGOs provide direct service. But others specialize in trafficking information. The most comprehensive NGOs do both and even more if necessary. And sometimes there's a progressive led-NGO that sets up a collaborative network of related nonprofit and grassroots organizations in a joint effort to find solutions to a given problem. But this is not always the case. Even in the teaching of human rights there's seldom a holistic framework. Students studying in law programs or in political science fields are often trained in specific human rights disciplines without a comprehensive model that embraces many different responses at the same time. Much of the skepticism surrounding human rights can be attributed to failed responses, but rarely does the public realize the entire scope of related human rights sectors. A documentary film about homelessness can only do so much. But in concert with the full range of human rights initiatives, the impact is far greater.

Human rights and peace education are also related to representation. The concept of education used here is broad because education happens in both formal schooling and via informal NGO networks. There's scarcely a major human rights NGO that doesn't work on education initiatives these days. Education also includes the dissemination of human rights information that occurs mostly over the Internet. While information such as recent reports by Human Rights Watch, is also representation, there's often an educative component to human rights Web sites that is missing in mainstream media representations. The critical difference between representation and education is that the former is about the transfer of knowledge and the latter is about the learning process, in both the academic and the social sense. This critical distinction is similar to the difference between peace studies and peace education. Peace studies are also about knowledge. But peace education, which embraces all human rights education initiatives, enables learners to not only understand the systemic and current obstacles to peace and justice, but more importantly, peace education helps develop skills to change and transform the problem.

The Documentary Tradition and Human Rights

The role of representation is intimately related to all of the various facets of human rights mentioned above. But as a peace educator, I am more interested in its relationship with the learning process. For this essay, documentary films will be the representational mode of choice. In recent years, the social documentary tradition has been experiencing a renaissance of sorts as nonfiction films are increasingly achieving notoriety and competing with feature films in theaters. Moreover, this is the only specific form of human rights representation that currently enjoys its own international festivals.

The study of documentary practice is rich and there exists a sizable literature on the ethics of representation, the different modes of representation, the tension between realism, objectivity, and subjectivity, and its relationship to ethnographic and experimental nonfiction films. There is no shortage of ideas for filmmaking. But the reception of documentary films by viewers is another matter. Outside of film reviews, usually done by a single viewer, there is little information on how collective viewers experience documentary films. Moreover, many documentary films are made to shine a light on a social problem, and the study of how the emerging field of human rights films stimulates collective activism is another lingering question.

What distinguishes a human rights film from another film is the exposure of serious violations reflected in the international standards. The film does not need to explicitly refer to human rights. Just the fact that the film represents social wrongs can be enough. For example, a serious documentary film about street kids is a human rights film by the sheer fact that children are protected through international human rights law. A film about domestic violence, even if it's a fictional feature film, can also be a human rights film because of the many international standards that protect women from violence.

As suggestive as is it to analyze feature films in human rights terms, more often than not, it's documentary films which garner the most attention in the human rights movement. We might assume here that a documentary film exposing a human rights situation has the potential to provide three valuable services. First, the work is a piece of research. As a visual human rights report, it may consist of evidence needed for legal proceedings. The film may also accompany traditional written appeals for changes in human rights policies and laws. The work can also contradict versions of human rights performance reported by offending governments. And most importantly, the film disseminates information and creates awareness about the issue.

Second, the film may be a form of action intended to change the situation at hand. Comprehensive human rights campaigns always need concrete forms of representation as part of an integrated action plan. From a "negative peace" perspective, films can be used as a deterrence to further abuse. Negative peace is action attempted to quell any immediate violence. Whatever it takes to stop the violence and prevent it from recurring is a negative peace strategy. "Positive peace" is more about setting up the conditions in the future for a culture of peace to exist in the first place. But a documentary film about a human rights issue is more akin to negative peace strategy because it bears witness to violence and suggests ways to render the situation. Quite often, films explicitly call for policy recommendations, and they facilitate those who do respond to the situation with a visible resource.

But to what extent does a film work in the service of positive peace? Strategies for positive peace are more pedagogical, future-oriented, and transformative. The third service a film may provide, then, is transformation. To be sure, it's a rare film that slips into a mode of proactive human rights or peace education that fuses knowledge, action, and transformation into one form of representation. More often than not, an educator has to use a human rights film in conjunction with a peace education pedagogy to create social transformation. But documentary films often accelerate the learning process and enhance whatever pedagogy is used for change. Following this line of thought, let's examine a couple of films in a concrete educational setting for their multiple roles and especially their educational potential for transformative learning.

Brazil as a Case Study

The role of representation within the human rights movement presents a holistic vision of human rights action that can be taught over the course of a semester. But this approach also needs to be modeled outside of the classroom in real time. For the last seven years, I've taken my students from New York to Rio de Janeiro for an intensive summer-abroad course. Brazil presents a fascinating example of the emerging field of international human rights study. Although Brazil has a history of violating a broad range of human rights, the last decade has brought about substantial constitutional, legislative, and institutional changes in respect for human rights. These changes include governmental support of human rights groups to investigate and report their findings, and new legal guarantees promoting freedom for political rights and freedom of speech and press. But at the local level, especially in large urban areas such as Rio, the challenges of human rights and peace work remain many, considering the continuing prevalence of poverty, crime, illiteracy, street children, child labor, child prostitution, police brutality, abusive prison conditions, and judicial corruption. The intention of this course is not to focus exclusively on the history of these violations, but to study the many positive responses and programs that have emerged to change social conditions and promote human rights and peace.

The month-long course is street-based, meaning that classes are held with various human rights projects in *favela* (shanty town) communities so that students can study the everyday practice of human rights. Thematically, the course covers many of the most pressing issues in Brazil, violence and public safety, women's human rights, children's rights, housing and community development, and many other areas. But underneath these violations is a base of poverty, and many Brazilians believe that economic human rights are the most important set of rights. In an effort to cover economic issues, we have visited NGOs implementing community programs that range from micro-credit lending to youth entrepreneurship projects.

Much as the course is about the practice of human rights in the streets, it's also important to introduce students to local advocates who are using representation. Each year, I always screen a few documentary films that are grouped into an overarching theme to help amplify a particular set of issues. Two years ago, the theme was economic human rights in Brazil. Since my course is based in the city, films also provide a means to introduce some of the most important rural human rights issues in Brazil. As in the city, the violations in the country are grave, and they echo the international standards for economic human rights.

These rights include the right to work; the right to dignified, creative, and productive labor; freedom of association; freedom from forced labor; safe working conditions; equal pay for equal work; the right to an adequate standard of living; the right for the protection of the child from economic exploitation; the right to education and access to information; the right to productive resources including land, and the right for indigenous peoples to manage and safeguard their natural resources and to use lands to which they have traditionally had access for subsistence.

These universal rights are the very human rights problems that exist today in Brazil. It's not surprising that these issues end up as themes and subthemes for many feature and documentary films. In fact, two of the most famous Brazilian feature films of all time, Hector Babenco's harrowing film *Pixote* (1980) and Walter Salles's Oscar nominee *Central Station* (1998), both portrayed the perils of economic survival in the desperate world of street children.[1] But economic human rights have also become the main subject of recent documentary films in Brazil.

The Scavengers

Of all the filmmakers in Brazil, one of the most internationally acclaimed is Eduardo Coutinho, who has chronicled the social landscape for the past four decades. When we visited Coutinho at his office, I asked if he would screen his award-winning 1992 documentary *Boca de Lixo* (Mouth of Garbage), known in English as *The Scavengers*.[2] In recent years, this film has continued to play in various international venues such as Cinema Novo film retrospectives at the Museum of Modern Art and the Guggenheim Museum in New York. These settings are quite a contrast from the shooting location at the immense Itaoca garbage dump outside Rio de Janeiro. Like many urban trash heaps around the world, Itaoca is not the end point for waste but an everyday workplace where scavengers pick through the rubbish for bottles and cans, cardboard and plastic, clothes and appliances, swill for animals and unspoiled food for themselves. Coutinho's style avoids narration for a strategy of reflexivity, which calls attention to the intervention and the production of the filmmaking process. Thus the film opens with the alarmed scavengers turning away from the video cameras, covering their faces, and gesturing that they have no desire to be filmed.

This setup creates a narrative strategy for Coutinho to eventually convince five workers to talk, and as they slowly warm to his questions, five lives unfold against a backdrop of work, poverty, and the outstretched arms of the Christ of Corcovado statue in the distance. The work consists of fighting for position when the trucks arrive, standing knee high in garbage, sifting through the waste with pitchforks, opening bags with bare hands, separating the salvageable, sorting recyclables, carrying heavy sacks and baskets, weighing the scrap, and negotiating with middlemen where money is finally exchanged. One scene captured a group of children in the middle of a noxious cloud, burning rubber off wires for the copper.

When the camera zooms in on the garbage, there's everything one can imagine, including medical waste. The scavengers mention that they sometimes even find "newborns" dumped from the trucks. When Coutinho corners one woman who was pricked with a hypodermic needle in the foot, she puts up an angry front. He asks how long she has worked at Itaoca and she confesses that she was born there on a piece of cardboard and that she's worked the heap her whole life. Coutinho eventually follows her home where her seven children, husband, and mother are presented. A different person away from the dump, she sheds her scavenger stigma and exudes a proud maternal dignity, an unending faith in God, and a thankfulness that garbage is supporting her family.

The transformation of each worker from the dump to his or her home is the key to this film. In each case, an anonymous person picking through garbage is endowed with dignity and integrity. Unlike most human rights films, which portray people simply as victims, this extended personification is what ultimately makes *The Scavengers* a richer and more compelling film. There's a wonderful scene in which Coutinho lines up a scavenger and her family to face the camera and as he holds the extended take their grim faces eventually crack up into laughter. What we learn about the workers are their hopes, their memories, their passions, their sense of humor, and their proud work ethic. Although everyone was poor, the scavengers all made a point of favorably comparing their lot with beggars and thieves. We also learn that most of the scavengers represent a continuum on the history of manual labor in Brazil. Traveling the country in search of work, they've planted coffee, cut sugarcane, fished for crabs, tapped rubber, harvested crops, drove trucks, worked as maids, and worked as construction workers.

As viewers (among those who can afford to choose their work) *The Scavengers* was an unsettling film for the class. And we were not quite sure what to do about it. Coutinho offers no solutions. And the film's generous humanism left us feeling less implicated as part of the problem. Only a couple of my students found the film exploitative. Most were simply awestruck by the actual film and the grim situation on the trash heap. In the spirit of community cinema, Coutinho ends the film by setting up a VCR in the middle of the dump. As the camera pans the scavengers, there's a genuine sense of wonderment among their faces as they watch themselves. But there are no illusions here. The screening passes and the film concludes with a dark specter of vultures waiting at the dump and a silhouette of workers combing through the debris. Like many recent documentaries in a human rights mode, *The Scavengers* presents the flip side of globalization and the other side of Rio that the world (including most Brazilians) almost never sees.

The Charcoal People

Away from the city, there's a different set of economic violations in rural Brazil that are even more removed from public perception. Another film I screened was *Os Carvoeiros* (1999), known in English as *The Charcoal People*.[3] Although directed by Academy Award-winning director Nigel Noble, working out of New York, it was a joint Brazilian production that was largely inspired by the Brazilian photographer Marcos Prado's book about the charcoal workers.[4]

While Prado's study was done in the fine arts documentary mode with rich black-and-white photographs, *The Charcoal People* was shot with super 16-mm color stock. But it's not a very colorful film, given the setting. Shot mostly in the scrub savannas in the Mato Grosso region of central Brazil, the film opens with a shot of thick chains being tied around tree trunks and attached to a tractor, which pulls the trees right out of the ground. The wood is then cut and taken to the charcoal camps where rows of smoking kilns are lined up to transform raw wood into chunks of black charcoal. The kilns themselves are as photogenic in the film as they appear in Prado's photographs. Made out of brick and mud, the large round structures (about the size of a small room) have a sculptural beauty rivaling the best vernacular architecture anywhere in the world. Shot in *cinéma vérité* style, Noble directs the cameras around the kilns to capture the wood chopping, the stacking, the building of the kilns, the exterior glazing with mud, the stoking of the fires, the burning, the bagging of charcoal, and the loading of the trucks. The work is as primitive as the charcoal camps themselves. But we quickly learn that the overflowing 18-wheelers pulling out of the camp's dirt tracks are headed for the multi-international steel mills in Minas Gerais where pig iron is exported around the world. Because pig iron is a combination of iron and charcoal, it takes an enormous amount of charcoal to keep the exports flowing. It's now estimated that there are sixty thousand charcoal workers spread out in the Brazilian interior, cutting trees and burning wood.

Like Coutinho, Nigel Noble follows a handful of workers through interviews and voice-overs. As each man tells his story, similar threads emerge such as the constant migration throughout Brazil following the camps which move in search of more trees. We also learn that nearly every one of the charcoal workers started as children and none of them can read or write. In fact, each *carvoeiro* blames his lot on a lack of education with the refrain that making charcoal is all they know how to do. Curiously, only one worker in the film discussed the coercion surrounding the camps. He explained that he and his son had to eventually escape to a different camp because they were stuck in a never ending cycle of debt bondage.

The line between coerced labor and what is known as contemporary slavery is very thin when it comes to making charcoal in Brazil. Several investigative reports, most notably Kevin Bales' study, *Disposable People: New Slavery in the Global Economy* (1999), have exposed how poor laborers are recruited throughout Brazil, promised stable work and wages, only to be taken to remote camps where their labor cards and their precious identity cards are held as ransom.[5] Paychecks never come because labor is always subtracted from the cost of transporting the laborers to the camps, their lodgings, their food, their tools, and any medicine—all at inflated prices.

Although Noble's film does not shift to these issues, he does cover the ecological violence inherent to charcoal production as his crew moves north at the end of the film. There are now 11 pig iron mills in the Amazon Rain Forest, with more on the way. Aerial views of cleared smoldering landscapes in the Amazon are heartbreaking. After cutting down an old grown tree with a chain saw, a worker admits with remorse: "That tree was over 100 years old and it only took five minutes to cut it down. But we have to survive so we're forced to do it." Unlike Coutinho's film, there's little room for hope or even humor in this picture. *The Charcoal People* closes with footage of young boys working at a camp, mixing glaze for the bricks, wheeling the heavy loads to the kilns, and applying the mud by hand. When asked how much he makes glazing kilns, an eight-year-old boy pauses and says he charges $1 a kiln and that if he works without stopping, he can cover two kilns in a day.

Films Seeding Peace Education

As documentary films, *The Scavengers* and *The Charcoal People* are two examples of what is now known as human rights films. They've fared better than most because each film has traveled the international festival circuit, they've had theatrical runs even in New York, and they exist in video and DVD format for rental. But even with wide distribution, it's still an open question as to how much effect each film has made on the situation they represent, especially because both films shy away from overt policy recommendations.

But these films do not exist in a vacuum. Each film is part of a larger discussion about universal economic human rights. Surrounding each film are also local advocates and NGOs working for specific social change related to the issues in each film. These groups often rely on international donor support, and representation is a key element in developing critical consciousness and mobilizing global solidarity. These local and international connections are the unintended consequences of globalization, and they also signal the growing movement of transnational human rights films.

When we were talking with the director Eduardo Coutinho after screening his film, the students were as curious about his filmmaking techniques as they were about his NGO, CECIP (Centro de Criacao de Imagem Popular), which Coutinho started in order to foster community-based media for citizenship and human rights.[6] Related to the international movement of human rights films around the world is the emergence of NGOs empowering people traditionally lacking a voice to represent themselves and respond to their own problems.

Many NGOs today are seeding advocacy through training and education in visual representation. The international organization Witness, for example, conducts trainings and workshops worldwide on video advocacy so that frontline human rights defenders can use various forms of media as tools for justice.[7] The Witness video workshops and manuals are intended to strengthen local capacity and self-sufficiency for human rights representation. Another example is Educational Video Center (EVC) in New York.[8] EVC is a media arts center that teaches documentary film production to "at-risk" youth. Production classes are combined with workshops in media literacy, public speaking, and work preparation skills. EVC also now trains educators in video production so they can set up portable workstations in their respective schools. The teachers then use video production in their classes as a means of discovering local generative themes in their own communities.

During the spring semester of 2000, I followed one of the teachers trained by EVC at an alternative high school in the community of Bushwick in Brooklyn. The teacher's name was Ellie Weiss, and she was running a class on community history/video production that counted for a social studies credit. Students taking the course had to go out and make films about the social history of their neighborhood. Given that Bushwick is one of the poorest and most troubled parts of New York, it was no surprise that the students chose to make their films about graffiti murals commemorating homicide victims, the legacy of arson and housing abandonment, teenage pregnancy, the crack cocaine epidemic, and gang warfare in Brooklyn. In the process of making films, students were becoming historians of their own neighborhood, reappropriating their own identities, and reconfiguring how they acquire knowledge. Back in the classroom, Weiss was using their video footage as a means of discussing the social ecology of violence. She was also teaching the students to think critically about nonviolence and social change.

As a learning tool, a film can be locally made or reflect a distant reality such as the films screened in Brazil. In the hands of the right educator using a progressive peace education pedagogy, a documentary film may have certain tangible advantages over more traditional forms of source material. First, a documentary film helps students visualize the situation in concrete terms. Visualization in turn can bring an immediacy to the situation and a sense that the film is presenting important news. Even if the film is cast in a retrospective mode, the film can evoke the sense of history in the making. I know from experience that teaching about contemporary slavery in rural Brazil through articles and human rights reports is not as engaging as is it when we begin with a documentary film about charcoal workers. The film sets up a learning process that transcends an abstract intellectual approach. The representation of real people's lives can generate a visceral connection and an emotive response from students, which is key, if the pedagogy hopes to develop the foundational values of peace education such as care, hope, empathy, tolerance, gender sensitivity, and a critical awareness of violence.

If violence is at the heart of human rights films, then documentaries about violations are, more often than not, a representation of tragedy. While there certainly are documentary films that celebrate struggles overcome, the collective realization of rights, and heroic figures who fought for social justice, the majority of human rights films are made in the tragic mode. Tragedy, in its classical theatrical sense, is the idea that dramatic characters can crystallize some central dynamics that are present in society. Distilled in the human rights narrative is conflict, the various manifestations of violence, and the many social forces that have affected how conflict is managed. This complex of violence then, is the problematic to be explored through further education. Problematization is extremely useful here because this strategy has little to do with problem solving. In peace education, to problematize a situation is to open it up with additional questions concerning the reasons for violence and the obstacles to peace.

From a pedagogical perspective, peace education is not about what you teach but how teaching and learning unfold together. This balance is inspired by the work of the late Brazilian educator Paulo Freire, who has become one of the patron saints of human rights and peace education.[9] Freire's insistence that education must lead to critical consciousness and social transformation has inspired the international movement for transformational education. Freire's themes of critical literacy, the analysis of power and systemic oppression, desocialization of regressive social values, advocacy and research, and self-education have supported the most progressive forms of human rights and peace education.

Taking the two films again as a case study, we might begin by locating the "generative themes" for each situation. For Freire, generative subjects convey words, experiences, situations, relationships, and, in this case, violations of human rights, which are problematized in an educational setting. Given the films' subject, the generative themes that we discussed as a class were related to the very violations or standards associated with economic human rights such as the right to safe working conditions; protection from forced labor; the right to education including vocational training; the right to receive fair wages that contribute to an adequate standard of living; the human right to unemployment protection; the right to reasonable limitation of working hours, rest, and leisure, and many other issues concerning work and workers.

In peace education, these generative themes or human rights standards serve as conceptual frameworks or a set of core organizing ideas used to begin a discussion about justice, critical knowledge, and social change.[10] In a mutually created dialogue, students pose inquires about these issues, reflect on their relationship to everyday life, and envision change. Again, our goal was not to come to any definitive conclusions. Simply naming the relative human rights standards, such as the rights that protect children from hazardous labor, has a way of closing down the discussion. But creating additional inquiries about harmful work opens up more pedagogical possibilities. Usually, this student-centered pedagogy is thought of as a "bottom up" approach, as opposed to a "top-down" model where information and policy recommendations are delivered from an authoritative expert.

Another way to approach a human rights film, besides discussing generative themes, is to map the conflict. Essentially, the strategy is to construct a learning matrix around a few general inquiries such as the following: What is this conflict about? Who are the actors in this conflict? What different perspectives exist on this conflict? What is happening at the various levels of society on this conflict? If we were to choose the first question concerning the nature of the conflict, we would construct a grid diagram to map this question. Running down the left-hand side, the educator could list the various human rights violations. Running left to right on the top, the facilitator could write the various social actors, such as personal, community, national, regional, and global. Mapping the issues, one could choose on the left side one of the many violations such as child labor exposed in *The Charcoal People*, and cross-reference it with different social actors. After discussing child labor with, say, the reference point of national or the State of Brazil, students would have to write their thoughts about child labor and Brazil at this particular nodal point on the map. By mapping each issue, students would more fully understand how human rights violations affect various levels of society. Students could then construct a second grid with the same violations and social actors and envision for each matrix what could be done to change the situation. A third grid could also be made to actually map at each stage who is already responding and working for justice and peace.

Developing the capacities for media literacy and self-education/ organization are two crucial goals of comprehensive peace education. These initiatives to change traditional teaching and learning relation-ships evoke what Paulo Freire called in Portuguese *conscientizacao*, or the collective critical consciousness needed for social transformation. In the EVC classes in the Brooklyn high school, students were actualizing Freire's notion of "praxis," which is action and reflection on the world in order to change it. Freirean pedagogy complements both the making and the studying of film because it's participatory, situated in a realist documentary mode, critical in the sense that the analysis encourages self-reflection and social reflection, democratic because everyone can construct knowledge, research-oriented, allowing students to pose inquiries about violence and activist where students envision change and map concrete strategies to move toward transformation.

Many human rights films today have informative Web sites where the public can learn more about the issues portrayed in the film. But additional knowledge is not necessarily education. Many filmmakers are now looking to extend the viewing-life of their films by creating educational lessons and guides to be used with the films in schools or in nonformal education settings. For the past few years, I've been teaching a human rights curriculum class where we begin with a documentary film as the centerpiece of design strategy. Placing the film in the center of the module allows for an organic sequence of lessons to build the-matically around the issues. The target age-group for our projects is young adults, late middle school through early college. The curriculum stresses that human rights are the underlying values and the conceptual frameworks needed to understand the particular curriculum. In the long run, this process perspective is more important than the actual content of the module or the film because of the many potential themes one has to negotiate as a student of peace education. In other words, a particular theme such as economic human rights in Brazil is not as important as learning the skills and capacities to read the world through a human rights lens.

Although we have not used *The Scavengers* or *The Charcoal People* as a central film in our curriculum projects, they would both work well within an overall framework of economic human rights. Both films are very rich and suggestive of the need to make holistic interrelationships between all human rights standards. Working with teams of graduate students, we've created high school curriculums for issues such as the trafficking of illicit diamonds out of Sierra Leone, child labor in Bangladesh, and small arms disarmament in Brazil. Although the projects are built around documentary films set in specific locations, the sweep of the curriculum is global. Various components of the curriculum include interactive lessons on human rights, media literacy, student research projects on the theme of the curriculum, and developmentally appropriate activism. The key to these projects is the film, which centers the teaching and learning, makes it real, and provides a reference point for progressive educational practices involving human rights, peace, and social change. This future, positive peace mode not only extends the life of a documentary film, but it fuses knowledge and action with a pedagogy of possibility.

Notes

1. *Pixote*. 1980. Directed by Hector Babenco. New Yorker Films. Central Station. 1988. Directed by Walter Salles. Columbia/Tristar Studios.
2. *The Scavengers*. 1992. Directed by Eduardo Coutinho. CECIP Films.
3. *The Charcoal People*. 2001. Directed by Nigel Noble. Vanguard Films.
4. Marcos Prado. 1999. *Os Carvoeiros*. (Self-Published).
5. Kevin Bales. 1999. *Disposable People: New Slavery in the Global Economy*. Berkeley: University of California Press.
6. For more information on CECIP, see their homepage: www.cecip.com.br
7. For more information on Witness, see: www.witness.org
8. For information on Educational Video Center, see: www.evc.org

9. Paulo Freire. 1970. *Pedagogy of the Oppressed*. New York: Continuum. Also see: Paulo Freire. 1973. *Education for Critical Consciousness*. New York: Continuum.

10. For more on human rights as conceptual frameworks in peace education, see: Betty A. Reardon. 2001. *Education for a Culture of Peace in a Gender Perspective*. Paris: UNESCO Publishing.

Chapter Six

Always on Top of the Food Chain—"Circle of Life," *The Lion King*, and Hegemony

SUN, CHYNG FENG

Children from the age range of 8–8 spend 44.5 hours per week watching TV, playing video games … listening to music, etc. This is more time than they spend with their parents (17 hours) or at school (30 hours).

—KAISER FAMILY FOUNDATION (2005)

The above statistics clearly demonstrate the significant role that the mass media have played in children's lives. That phenomenon has been exploited by advertisers to create a teen market that has risen in numbers from 6.1 billion in 1989 to 30 billion in 2002, a nearly fivefold increase (Schor, 2004, p. 23). As a college professor of media studies, I daily encounter students who are sophisticated in media technology but uncritical in decoding media texts. Even though they carry all kinds of brand names on their clothing and discuss the previous night's TV shows with enthusiasm, they strongly resist the idea that media have a significant influence on them. It seems an insult to their intelligence and independence, as well as an offence to this "greatest democracy in the world," that media can serve as a brainwashing machine that alters their minds. In fact, these students are not wrong about their suspicion of the myth that media are like "hypodermic needles" that inject messages into their brains and change their perceptions. As audience research theories and empirical research have reasoned, media affect us in much more indirect, subtle, and long-term ways. Furthermore, media may have the biggest impact in our societies not by changing our preconceived notions of the world but by reinforcing them; in the process, the media make change impossible to imagine and thus impossible to occur (Shanahan & Morgan, 1999). As cultivation analysis scholars convincingly demonstrate in the "mainstreaming effect," people who view a lot of television tend to have a similar world view that is consistent with the dominant ideologies perpetuated on TV, regardless of their race, class, gender, religious and political affiliations (Gerbner, Gross, Morgan, & Signorielli, 2000).

In this essay, I will first argue that using a cultural studies approach to teach media will help students develop a contextual and holistic understanding of the media. I will then introduce the Gramscian concept of "hegemony" that is crucial to explaining media's role in perpetuating elite interests that are encoded in media messages and disseminated by media outlets. Lastly, I will use Disney's *The Lion King* to explain how hegemony operates in the "lion's kingdom" in the film itself, as evidenced in the relationships between the lions and their subordinated animals. Furthermore, I will demonstrate the role that hegemony plays when audiences use "commonsense" to interpret the movie text, an analysis that will reveal how hegemony functions in the larger societal context.

Cultural Studies Approach

Educators who are tuned into popular culture understand that the ostrich-like approach of "just say no" or "turn off the TV" will not work with their students. They recognize the urgent need to teach young people about media. Thus, there has been an explosion of curricula and practices for media literacy in the 1990s; nonetheless, different approaches and disagreements have created tension among educators and have interfered with collaborative and broad-base support for media literacy

(Hobbs, 1998, p. 16). Moreover, some media scholars celebrate the audiences' creative readings and usage of the media, undermining the possible media impact on the audience (Jenkins, 2000).

As Kelvin Sealey indicates in the introduction of this book, it has long been an interest and concern for educators to apply cultural studies in the classroom. Being a college professor in media studies who uses a critical cultural studies approach, I will argue that cultural studies is inherently political. As Kellner (2003) states: "There is an intrinsically critical and political dimension to the project of cultural studies that distinguishes it from objectivist and apolitical academic approaches to the study of culture and society" (p. 11). Cultural Studies' genealogy is deeply rooted in Marxism as evidenced by the works of its British Jamaican founder Stuart Hall who wrestled with classical Marxism, the French Marxist Louis Althusser, and the Italian Marxist Antonio Gramsci (Hall, 1996). One does violence to cultural studies not only when one detaches media representations from their material base and from the interests that they serve, but also when one removes the application of media education from its potential for creating a more democratic media system, and arguably, a more democratic society. Protesting the "conflation of media literacy and activism," some media literacy educators advocate for a purely "textual base" analysis and emphasize that the goal of media literacy should be to "promote autonomy through the development of analysis, reasoning, communication and self-expression skills" (Hobbs, 1996, p. iii). The problem of this "textual base" approach that Hobbs promotes, as Jhally and Lewis (1998) point out, is that media education needs to be "contextual" in order to cultivate concerned citizens rather than smart consumers who can differentiate and then choose good media products from the bad ones (p. 112). Educators such as those who employ Hobb's depoliticization of media analysis are indicative of a much larger political disengagement in this country.

Jhally and Lewis's vision is supported by Kellner (2003) when he advocates the use of a cultural studies approach to understand media; this method encompasses three elements: political economy, content, and the audience. With different terms, Gerbner (1999) uses almost identical concepts in his design of the Cultural Indicators Project in 1976, insisting on a three-pronged approach: institutional policy analysis (political economy), message system (content analysis), and cultivation analysis (audience, media effects).

Hegemony is particularly important to understand the tension between the dominant ideology propagated by mainstream media and the audience's individual agency; this theory also is crucial to our investigation of why, despite undermining the audience's self interest, the ideology that maintains the status quo often prevails. Developed by Italian Marxist Antonio Gramsci in the 1930s, hegemony explains the important role that culture and media have played in securing the consent of subordinated groups. Gramsci has undertaken a crucial theoretical development based on Marx's base/super structure model, making it much more applicable to a contemporary capitalist and electoral democracy such as the United States.

Super/Base Structure

In Marx's classical "base and superstructure" model, in a social formation the mode and relations of production (the material base) ultimately determine the world of ideas (the superstructure that includes legal, political, and cultural institutions, as well as ideas and consciousness). Marx states:

> In the social production of their existence, men inevitably enter into definite relationships, which are independent of their will, namely relations of production … the totality of these relations of production constitutes the economic structure of society, the real foundation, on which arises a legal and political superstructure and to which correspond definite forms of social consciousness. The mode of production of material life conditions the general process of social, political and intellectual life. (cited in Hall, 1977, p. 47)

Marx's formulation helps us to see that ideas are not free-floating; rather, they have their material entities and serve certain interests over others. This model, however, assumes that ideas are merely the reflections of the determining material base and implies a "necessary correspondence" between social-economic and ideological spheres; thus, the economic base guarantees certain ideological outcomes and implies that certain ideas belong only to certain classes of people. This rigid model denies the possibility that ideas may have their own effectiveness and may provide change. This framework also fails to explain the different forms of consciousness apparent in society. Within the same class, many ideas exist and sometimes oppose each other. Different classes often share the same ideology; "patriotism" is certainly an ideology that cements different classes in the United States but varies in terms of how it is articulated within each social class.

Even though the super/base structure may be reductive, it is undeniable that in order for a stratified and unequal society to function in a relatively peaceful condition, certain ideologies dominate and thus help to cement the different social strata with their conflicting or even oppositional interests.

Marx and Engels further explain that the "ruling ideology" becomes the dominant ideology for the entire society as a result of the elites' control over the means of the material as well as mental production. Marx and Engels (1970) state that:

> The ideas of the ruling class are in every epoch the ruling ideas, i.e., the class which is the ruling material force of society, is at the same time its ruling intellectual force. The class which has the means of material production at its disposal has control at the same time over the means of mental production, so that thereby generally speaking, the ideas of those who lack the means of mental production are subject to it. The ruling ideas are nothing more than the ideal expression of the dominant material relationships, the dominant material relationships grasped as ideas; hence the relationships which make the one class the ruling one, therefore, the ideas of its dominance. (p. 64)

Marx and Engels suggest that when the ruling class controls the means of mental production, they also control the result of the production, that is, the ideas. Marx and Engels, however, fail to explain the process of how the ideas that further the interests of the elite get disseminated, perpetuated, and eventually accepted by the subordinated group. It is important to note that the ruling ideology will not be effective if the populace does not consent to it. If we believe in human subjectivity and agency, why and how would the oppressed accept such ideologies that undermine their own interests?

One of the major problems with Marxism is that it assumes the nature of ideology in relation to class instead of investigating how the ideology interacts with class, gender, race, sexualities, and other social categories in multiple and complex ways. It also fails to examine how ideology is constructed through and by the text, and how it is articulated in the formation of identity. Both analyses are crucial in understanding U.S. society in which "American Dream"—that the United States is a fair and just meritocracy and all its citizens can achieve whatever they want if they work hard—is the dominant ideology. In this context, it is difficult for people to accept the existence of a "ruling class." Hegemony helps us to understand the role that media play in U.S. society in two ways: firstly, in terms of the strategies that the ruling elites' use to control the society; and secondly, in terms of the participation of the oppressed that further secures that control.

Hegemony

Gramsci (1971) states that the ruling class controls the society by dominating its antagonistic groups with overt force (such as by means of the police or military); at the same time, the ruling class leads other subordinated groups by actively seeking their consent and by representing itself as morally, intellectually, and economically superior. Hegemony is the process by which the powerful seek consent by articulating, and incorporating, the interests of the oppressed. At times, however, the ruling class does make certain sacrifices in order to form "compromise equilibrium" (p. 161); such sacrifice cannot hurt the essence of the ruling class because even though it poses itself as the moral and political leader, its power is fundamentally economic. Most importantly, the hegemonic class persuades the populace that the social and economic system that oppresses them is benevolent, natural, fixed, and cannot be changed (Dines & Humez, 2003, p. 731).

Gramsci (1971) believes that the most powerful tool that the ruling elite uses to "cement" the leaders and the followers is ideology. He believes that the State not only has and requests consent, but also "educates" this consent. This task, however, is most often left to the entities that carry out the private initiative of the ruling classes (p. 259). Educational, religious, and cultural organizations actively disseminate the ideology that affirms that the interests of both the ruling elite and its subordinates are one and the same. Still, in our twenty-first century, none of these entities is as important and far-reaching as the mass media.

Applying Boggs's and Nordenstreng's theories, Lull (2003) lays out the ways that media perpetuate the elites' wealth and power by introducing into individuals' consciousness elements that are commonly shared in a culture. The owners and managers of media companies have the particular advantage of controlling the content. Lull (1995) emphasizes that the media messages are often interlocked and reinforced by other social and culture values.

> Mass-mediated ideologies are corroborated and strengthened by an interlocking system of efficacious information-distributing agencies and taken-for-granted social practices that permeate every aspect social and cultural reality. Messages supportive of the status quo emanating from school, business, political organizations, trade unions, religious groups, the military, and the mass media all dovetail together ideologically. This inter-articulating, mutually reinforcing process of ideological influence is the essence of the hegemony. (p. 62)

As Lull further suggests, when similar messages are echoed in all spheres, they become automatic and transparent. They lose their origination, become "authorless," appear to be neutral, and achieve a universal and natural status; in other words, they become "commonsense." Gramsci (1971) describes commonsense as containing:

> Stone Age elements and principles of a more advanced science, prejudices from all past phases of history at the local level and intuitions of a future philosophy which will be that of a human race united the world over. (p. 324)

In other words, commonsense is an already formed and assumed terrain of fragmented and contradictory ideas that are accumulated historically. Gramsci further asserts that ideology is the essential tool for winning popular consent, and the struggle for hegemonic leadership is fought at the level of commonsense. High philosophy cannot achieve political effectiveness unless it connects with practical consciousness, and this articulation is achieved through directed political activity, not as an effect of economic determinacy.

Hegemony is one of the most important conceptual tools in cultural studies to examine not only the ways that media disseminate and perpetuate elitist interests but also the reasons why the subordinated group would adopt and act out certain beliefs that harm their own economic interests. Such seemingly irrational actions on the part of the less powerful were identified by Marx as "false consciousness." However, that conception implies that people are merely being duped by ideologies beyond their control, thus not placing much value on the populace's agency. Hegemony, by stressing active consent from the subordinated and incorporating their subjectivities, complicates the interaction between the dominant and the elite. One may argue that the oppressed act according to the dominant ideology that hurts them because they lack access to alternative ideologies; for these reasons, Gramsci emphasizes the importance of education and counter-hegemonic messages.

Most of my students, however, never have been exposed to a meaningful discussion of Marxist or socialist thoughts before they entered my class. Thus, my students often found the concept of hegemony to be counterintuitive and counter-commonsense, as well as too abstract and intangible to relate. I found Disney's *The Lion King* to be an excellent tool for helping students to appreciate the value of this theory by addressing two levels of hegemony: the first level is hegemony within the movie's narrative in terms of the relationships of the animals who live in the kingdom ruled by the Lion's monarchy, while the second level is demonstrated when the film "interpellates" the audience as subjects (Bobo, 2002) within a society permeated with "commonsense" that is used to justify a "white supremacist, patriarchal and capitalist hierarchy" (hooks, 1994).

The Lion King and Hegemony

"An instant classic!" declared James Carr (1994) of *The Boston Globe*. *The Lion King* (1994) was Disney's most successful animated film, both financially and critically. Its box office revenue grossed over 312 million dollars, which is the fifth highest gross among all movies before 1994 (Honeycutt, 13). Moreover, its video sold 32 million copies, even 5 million more than Disney's prediction (Hettrick, 1995), making it the number one seller in 1995 (Lee's Movie Info, 2004). When combined with revenues from box office, home videos, and 186 items of merchandising, *The Lion King* generated more than one billion dollars in profit (McChesney, 1999). In addition to its financial success, Disney also captured two Oscars and two Grammys for the film's music (Jolson-Colburn 5; Honeycutt 13). Lion King, however, is not without critics. Its depiction of the little Lion King witnessing his father's violent death raises concerns for very young audiences allowed in because of its G rating (Matchan, 1994). Reviewers also criticize its racist portrayals of hyenas as stereotypical urban poor blacks (Giroux, 1999; Gagnon, 1998; Palmer, 2000), its sexist depiction of a passive lioness (Foster, 1994), and its glorification of an unfair and unjust system (Newberger, 1994). But overall, *The Lion King* was praised for its technological breakthroughs (Carr, 1994), visual presentations (Carr, 1994), and its positive message embodied in a coming-of-age story in which the main character accepts his responsibilities and grows up (Matchan, 1994). Annalee R. Ward (1996) claims that Disney's animated films have tremendous reach throughout American popular culture and have become a "moral educator" (p. 171) Moreover, the film, by using a "mythical narrative" (p. 171) particularly fits that role. According to Ward (1996), *The Lion King* also contains a religious undertone, taken from biblical stories:

> For many of the myths that *The Lion King* draws from are religious, taken from biblical stories. They include the stories of Paradise, the Fall, the reign of Satan, the need for a savior, the cataclysmic destruction of the earth, and the return of the savior who restores peace and begins his reign as rightful king. (p. 172)

Contrary to Ward's celebration of *The Lion King*'s moral values that are upheld by the society as a whole in order to ensure harmony and peace, I argue that the morality propagated by the movie reflects an ideology that benefits the ruling elite while disempowering the subordinates. Most importantly, *The Lion King* is a perfect example with which to discuss how hegemony operates within and outside the film.

The opening scene of *The Lion King* is the celebration of the birth of the future king Simba. The royal couple lovingly gaze and kiss each other (conveniently forgetting that lions are not "monogamous" and they do not form nuclear families) as they sit high up on the top of "Pride Rock" with all the other animals waiting below. In a dramatic gesture, the shaman baboon raises Simba high up; at that precise moment, the cloud breaks up and rays of sunlight shine directly on the cub. The animals cheer, bowing their heads and saluting their new ruler.

Analyzing the old movie tradition, Richard Dyer (1997) observes that when the light is shown from above, it often suggests that the object is "virtuous" and "celestial" (p. 118); furthermore, this technique may be influenced by an old belief dating back to the twelfth century that says heaven is a place of light. For example, in *Uncle Tom's Cabin*, when an angel appears, she is bathed in rays of light from above (p. 119). It is thus apparent that the light that shines on Simba symbolizes that he is the "chosen one," and that he has some special innate quality that makes him the destined leader. Another apparent pattern of the usage of light throughout *The Lion King* is the association between light equaling good while dark is associated with evil. As Dyer (1997) observes in film representations:

> [w]hite as a symbol, especially when paired with black, seems more stable than white as a hue or skin tone. It remains firmly in place at the level of language—most people find themselves saying things like "everything has its dark side," "it's just a little white lie," and "that's a black mark against you"… the use of the oppositions in pictorial representation remains surprisingly widespread. (p. 60)

Dyer (1997) uses many examples to show that the filmmakers routinely assign dark features, such as darker skin and hair to "bad" characters while they give blonde hair and fair skin to the "good" characters (pp. 61–64). This is certainly the case for *The Lion King*. In the film, the characters are neatly divided into good and evil camps. The good ones include the lions and the animals that are obedient or friendly to the lions, such as antelopes, zebras, and Simba's friends who are a meerkat and a warthog; they all have bright and vibrant colors and live in places with light. The evil ones, such as Scar, who is the old king Mufasa's conniving brother, and the lowlife hyenas, are all darker skinned and live in caves and shadowy places. In addition, Scar speaks in a British accent, which evokes the sense of him being "archaic," "aloof," and "removed" from the masses. In the striking scene, in which Mufasa confronts Scar for not showing up at the ceremony to celebrate Simba's birth, we see these two brothers in the same frame, but one is bright and good while the other is dark and evil. The pattern seems too consistent to be accidental.

Most interesting about the opening scene is the question it begs to answer: Why would the animals be so overjoyed by the addition of yet another predator that might eat them up? Are they stupid or brainwashed? One may argue that the director merely took real world examples, such as when the British monarchy presented their new prince to the public or when the newly crowned Pope greeted worshipers. However, modeling an animal world on human societies precisely proves the point that cartoons are highly ideological, thus debunking the myth that they are merely innocent entertainment as Disney's defenders would want us to believe (Foster, 1994). If we apply the concept of hegemony, the animals have given their consent to the lion's monarchy and now accept the new lion as their future leader. Moreover, the reign over all the animals by this vulnerable and defenseless cub is presented as natural, determined, and destined, so much so that no questions are permitted. Nowhere is the lion's ruling ideology more clear than in "the circle of life," as explained in the following dialogue:

> Father: Look Simba, everything the light touches is our kingdom. ... One day, Simba, the sun will set on my time here, and will rise with you as the new king.
>
> Son: And this will all be mine?
>
> Father: Everything.
>
> Son: Everything the light touches? What about the shadowy places?
>
> Father: That's beyond our borders. You must never go there.
>
> Son: But I thought the king can do whatever he wants.
>
> Father: There's more to being king than getting your way all the time.
>
> Son: There is more?

> Father: Everything you see exists together in a delicate balance. As a king, you need to understand that balance and respect all the creatures, from the crawling ant to the leaping antelopes.
>
> Son: Dad, don't we eat the animals?
>
> Father: Yes. Let me explain. When we die, our bodies become the grass and the antelope will eat the grass. So, we are all connected in a great circle of life.

The father lion thus has explained how hegemony works. In order to earn consent, the elite sometimes may have to make sacrifices. Even though it is not clear what kind of sacrifice Lion Kings have to make, this give-and-take attitude is considered necessary by the ruler as the old lion explains that "There's more to being king than getting your way all the time," and "… respect all the creatures, from the crawling ant to the leaping antelopes." And it is exactly this willingness to curb one's desire that makes Mufasa the good king and Scar the bad king. Moreover, this dichotomy is made explicit when, later in the film, Scar arrogantly declares that because he is the king, he can do whatever he wants. Gramsci explains, however, that the sacrifice cannot cut to the economic core, because even though the ruling class's dominance is cultural and moral, it is still fundamentally economic. So even though *The Lion King* needs to "respect" the animals, they nonetheless eat them with no guilt.

In fact, in this "circle of life," lions' acts of killing and eating antelopes are not only rightful, natural, and necessary, but also benevolent and good for everyone; as the concept of hegemony indicates, the ruling class persuades the populace that their interests are one and the same. According to this logic, antelopes should really thank lions for eating them so that one day the lions can die and turn into grass so that future antelopes can eat the grass. (Along the same line of thinking, a student said that because *The Lion King* eats the weaker antelopes, survivors get to pass down the stronger genes, so it is better for the antelopes.) This type of reasoning is very similar to the religious doctrine that the poor are indeed luckier than the rich since their misery, caused by the rich, will ease their ascent to heaven., The father lion, Mufasa, tries to equate a lion's death with that of an antelope, so as to make them equals in society. However, as my students observed, the lion's death is a natural one while the antelopes suffer violent deaths that involve being hunted down and killed, with their lives being thus unnaturally and tragically shortened. Even though some reviewers praised *The Lion King* for its teaching of ecology lessons to the youth, the concept of the "circle of life" actually turns the concept of the food chain into a legitimatization of oppression. Lions are indeed meat eaters, but antelopes and all other animals are not automatically their food. Animals do not lie down, bow in respect and offer themselves for a lion's dinner. In fact, they run, they fight, and they struggle; if they are strong and in large groups, they may run away, hurt, or even kill the lion. Nothing therefore is indeed pre-determined, as the old Lion King declares. Animals are not ideological and do not respect the rules of hierarchy.

As Hall (1980) states in his seminal article on encoding/decoding, even though messages are polysemic and can be interpreted with different meanings, encoding will have the effect of "constructing some of the limits and parameters within which decodings will operate" (p. 135). We can use a metaphor to explain the idea of setting limits: the filmmaker is like a person who is holding a flashlight in a dark theater, and the audience can see only the objects on which the light shines. The things that are in the dark thus become off limits. In *The Lion King*, because the old Lion King was praised as a "great" king by his queen, his son, future daughter-in-law, as well as by his most obedient servant, the audience accepts this claim without any support, as evidenced in many of the reviews or summaries of this movie that refer to Mufasa as a "great king." Hyenas as a group, on the other hand, are doomed to a life of poverty, and it was never explained why the hyenas deserved to be banished to live in the elephants' graveyard while the lions enjoyed prosperity. Hyenas suffer the double bind that the oppressed often experience: you are forced to live in poverty, with no access to resources, and then you are blamed for being poor, all proof that you are lazy.

In no subtle way, hyenas are racialized through their dark skin, accents, and mannerisms as urban poor blacks. They are also depicted as stupid, lazy, and prone to violence. One hyena speaks in urban black slang (played by Whoopi Goldberg) while another utters Spanish words (played by Latino actor Cheech Marin who also played two Chihuahuas in Disney's *Oliver & Company* and *Lady and the Tramp*). When hyenas move to "Pride Lands," they soon overpopulate and deplete the resources and ghettoize the whole kingdom. Child psychologist Carolyn Newberger (1994) observes that it is the same racist rhetoric that blames the African-American urban poor for the United States' social decline. The defenders of *The Lion King* dismiss criticisms that the hyenas portrayal is racist and counter that Mufasa was played by African-American actor James Earl Jones. This indeed highlights the importance of analyzing media texts not solely in terms of each social category alone, such as race or gender, but in terms of the complex intersections among the different categories. James Earl Jones, a Tony Award winner, is known for his resonant basso voice and commanding presence; he certainly speaks standard English. It is precisely the difference between Jones and Goldberg's accents, mannerisms, and uses of languages that distinguishes what is an acceptable black from an unacceptable one.

Gramsci suggests that when the dominant class fails to lead with consent, they will dominate with force. It is evident that when Scar tries to steal the throne, he makes alliances with the hyenas, and in a chilling scene the militaristic hyenas march with goose-steps in a cave, which recalls the Hitler-worship in Triumph of the Will. But the benevolent rulers do not need to resort to violence. Simba's love interest Nala goes searching, finds him, and persuades him to take his rightful place as the king; interestingly, she never questions if she herself could become the leader. As soon as Simba defeats Scar and becomes the destined king, the "Pride Lands" miraculously regains its prosperity. It is precisely in this moment that we see an ideology that serves to legitimize the male lion's dominance: only the lion with the proper blood line and the proper gender, can be rightful ruler who benefits everyone.

Since this media text is indeed polysemic and audiences do react with different readings, I do not claim that my interpretation is the only one; I nevertheless will reason that the argument here is clearly articulated and embodied in the text. Furthermore, this film also presents an opportunity to discuss another level of hegemony: the hegemony that is built on a certain commonsense that allows the audience to agree with the ideology presented in the film, the same dominant ideology that benefits the elite in the actual society in which the audiences reside.

While I was producing the educational film *Mickey Mouse Monopoly: Disney, Childhood and Corporate Power* (Sun, 2001), I interviewed some college students who had taken a course on Disney's animated films and on their original story versions. A female student, who was raised by a mother who is a Disney fan, having seen Disney movies since before she could even talk, responded to my question regarding *The Lion King*'s racist portrayals of hyenas as urban blacks:

> I think you can read into a movie too much, something that's merely for entertainment value as what I see Disney to be … If you take it purely in the text of the movie, or in the text of the nature in general, hyenas are scavengers, they are outcasts, they are not generally liked by other animals, just by the nature of hyenas as an animal.

We can see how "nature" is evoked in her defense of Disney's portrayals and how much she relies on "commonsense" to prove her point. Another male student has watched *The Little Mermaid* more than fifty times and has often sang his favorite song in that movie at Christmas and at other family gatherings. When asked about his opinions on the criticism about sexism in Disney's film, he said, "I have to assume that Disney didn't do it on purpose … If you do things long enough … It is just how things are." This viewpoint again underscores that commonsense has become ideological-free, and as natural as "just how things are." I also asked another young woman if the critical analysis of Disney's films affected her enjoyment of her favorite Disney movies. She replied "no" and went on to explain thus: "I can look at a Disney movie as both entertainment, and the underlying psychological factors that they have—this is what the animators did and if they added it on purpose. Or I can just look at it as something fun, and I like to sing along and I love the story." Music is clearly an important element that draws the audience in, one more way to interpellate them. This student's separation of enjoyment and critical analysis was not unique either. In an audience research project conducted with this class, there were many students who claimed that they were utilizing the same processing (Sun & Scharrer, 2004). This finding suggests that if the audiences have emotional attachment to certain media texts and they are unwilling to let go of the pleasure, they will neither undertake a critical analysis nor accept the responsibility it brings and the challenges it poses. That is, they will not want to stand outside of hegemony because the alternative may be lonely and joyless. Carolyn Newberger, in my interview, compared Disney with Santa Claus; she asked, "If you say that there was no Santa Claus, would you return the gifts too?"

In her analysis of black women's viewing of *The Color Purple*, Jacqueline Bobo analyzes how certain texts draw in their readers/viewers to become the subjects:

> Interpellation is the way in which the subject is hailed by the text; it is the method by which ideological discourses constitute subjects and draw them into the text–subject relationship. John Fiske describes "hailing" as similar to hailing a cab. The viewer is hailed by a particular work; if he or she gives a corporative response to the beckoning, then not only is he or she constructed as a subject, but the text then becomes a text, in the sense that the subject begins to construct meaning from the work and is constructed by the work. (p. 218)

Then, how did *The Lion King* "hail" hundreds of thousands of people? The film appears to tap into our deepest and most universally shared emotions and yearnings. It is a story that can be read as the bond and love between a father and a son, as a coming-of-age story in which a youth grows up and accepts his responsibility, and as a story about pain, suffering, and eventual triumph and happiness. *The Lion King*'s message also makes sense for most people who are so accustomed to a hierarchical society that they see it as only natural and necessary to give their rulers consent in order to ensure the harmony and prosperity of the larger society. And most importantly, we have learned to identify with the ruler but not the ruled, the latter being the real positions in which most people exist.

The Lion King, like many popular Hollywood movies in the United States, also became a blockbuster internationally. What is the implication for this film and its ideology spreading throughout the globe? Wong (1999) applies hegemony in her analysis of *The Lion King*'s tremendous success in Hong Kong and states that "largely due to the cultural nurture, Hong Kong Chinese are very receptive to the ideologies projected in *The Lion King*" " because of the Confucius teaching of male dominance and class hierarchy" (pp. 8 & 9); moreover, the social psyche of the Hong

Kong Chinese is very much like the one depicted in *The Lion King*. It is interesting that in Wong's analysis, she fails to contemplate that since this film was even more popular in the United States, one might argue that the U.S. populace may embody the "social psyche" that makes *The Lion King*'s ideology feel particularly familiar and attractive. Or that the U.S. society also may resemble the one depicted in *The Lion King*. I will argue that the author's failure in questioning is precisely the demonstration of the power of U.S. hegemony overseas, particularly over the third world. The United States most often represents itself as the beacon of democracy and as a land of freedom and equality. Within this framework, it would be counter-commonsense that *The Lion King*'s world view could have any resemblance to that of U.S. society.

Conclusion

Hegemony is the process by which the ruling elite secures consent from its subordinates, but such consent is never earned once and for all; it requires constant reinforcement and there is always some room for resistance through subversive and counter-hegemonic cultural work (Dines & Humez, 2003). Precisely because of the tremendous effort, money, and energy spent on generating, disseminating, and legitimizing dominant messages in the mass media, we can understand how fragile hegemony must be and how the ruling ideology is in conflict with the populace's interests. Gramsci underscores the importance of the populace to recognize and counter hegemony; the first step is consciousness raising. He states:

> .... the starting-point of critical elaboration is the consciousness of what one really is, and is "knowing thyself" as a product of the historical process to date which has deposited in you an infinity of traces, without leaving an inventory. (Gramsci, 1971, p. 324)

Said (1978) indicates that the translator of the English version of *Selections from the Prison Notebook* left out the important phrase: "therefore, it is imperative at the outset to compile such an inventory" (p. 25). Gramsci sees critical self-examination as the first step for liberation: the condition when individuals become aware that they are part of a hegemonic force and thus can recognize that the dominant ideology that they used to believe actually undermines their own interests. With a "progressive self-consciousness," they may feel "different" and "independent," and in the process will be able to form a worldview that is critical, coherent, and counter-hegemonic (Gramsci, 1971, pp. 333–334).

Even though self-examination is important, we also should recognize that it is very difficult to have individuals undertake critical work when they are bombarded with dominant messages and have no access to well-thought-out and reasoned counter-hegemonic ideologies. Media content is often encoded in such a way that it makes certain readings easier to come up with, and the process of decoding is more enjoyable. Even though Fiske (1989) emphasizes the pleasure one experiences while coming up with resistant readings, Condit (1989) observes a pro-choice activist and an antiabortion activist watching a pro-choice TV program and concludes that it is more difficult and emotionally draining for the person who came up with oppositional readings than for the one with preferred readings. This observation seems to make immediate sense when considering everyday experiences. The act of disagreement with a mass media message is often frustrating and may leave individuals with a sense of powerlessness, because the process seems like having a stressful argument with another; what they do confront is not just one person, but rather an institution that they know disseminates the same message to hundreds of thousands of people. Furthermore, one needs to be able to *think* outside the frame that the text sets up in order to even "disagree," thus one needs to have prior access to alternative discourse as well as the concepts and vocabulary in order to make alternative readings. The difficulty of coming up with oppositional readings speaks to the importance of ensuring that counter-hegemonic messages be mass produced and mass distributed. We not only need to understand our media institutions and systems in order to demand that media companies be responsive to our interests, but we also need to teach our students to be critical thinkers and active citizens who advocate for alternative media. Here we go full-circle to the issue of media education: the discussion of hegemony further underscores the importance of using a cultural studies approach to utilize a holistic teaching strategy that addresses the analyses of political economy, textual analysis, and audience.

When we have media that no longer solely perpetuate, naturalize, and normalize a fixed hierarchy and a benevolent and necessary ruling class, we may see different kinds of antelopes: ones who would not bow to the newborn king nor consider themselves as a lion's inevitable meal, but rather would happily roam around the grasslands without someone else defining the "circle of life" for them.

Notes

It was in the summer of 1997 that I first heard of "hegemony" in Gail Dine's lecture at Wheelock College in Boston. It is not an exaggeration to say that the concept was like lightening that shed so much light on how the world works and on the role media play in that world. Thanks to Gail for her continuing support for my various intellectual and academic endeavors, including her insights on this essay. Thanks also to Fanny Rothschild for her editorial assistance. Thanks to Kelvin Shawn Sealey for his invitation and when he said, "The best of what we can be as scholars is to share with others—students and colleagues—what little access and power we have in the world. If what we do has value, the world will find ways to acknowledge that."

References

Bobo, J. (2002). The color purple: Black women as cultural readers. In R. M. Coleman (ed.), *Say It Loud: African-American Audiences, Media and Identity* (pp. 205–227). New York: Routledge.

Carr, J. (1994, June 24). The Lion King rules more tough-minded than sugarcoated. *The Boston Globe*, p. 47.

Condit, C. (1989). The rhetorical limits of polysemy. *Critical Studies in Mass Communication.* 6(2), 103–122.

Dines, G. & Humez, J. (Eds.). (2003). *Gender, Race and Class in Media* (2nd ed). Thousand Oaks, CA: Sage.

Dyer, R. (1997). *White*. New York: Routledge.

Fiske, J. (1989). Productive pleasures. *Understanding Popular Culture* (pp. 50–68). Boston: Unwin Hyman.

Foster, D. (1994, July 26). The "Lion King" falls prey to howls of sexism, racism. *Chicago Tribune*, p. 3.

Gagnon, M. K. (1998). *Race-ing Disney: Race and Culture in the Disney University*. Unpublished dissertation, Simon Fraser University.

Gerbner, G. (1999). Forward. In M. Morgan & J. Shanahan (eds.), *Television and Its Viewers: Cultivation Theory and Research* (pp. ix–xiii). Cambridge: Cambridge University Press.

Gerbner, G. Gross, L. Morgan, M. & Signorielli, N. (2000). Growing Up with Television: Cultivation Processes. In J. Bryant & D. Zillman (eds.), *Media Effects: Advances in Theory and Research* (2nd ed., pp. 43–67). Hillsdale, NJ: Erlbaum.

Giroux, H. (1999). *The Mouse That Roared: Disney and The End Of Innocence*. Lanham, MD: Rowman & Littlefield Publishers, Inc.

Gramsci, A. (1971). *Selections from the Prison Notebooks*. London: Lawrence & Wishart.

Hall, S. (1977). Rethinking the "Base and Superstructure" Metaphor. In J. Bloomfield et al. (eds.), *Class, Hegemony and Party* (pp. 43–72). London: Lawrence and Wishart.

Hall, S. (1980). Encoding/Decoding. In S. Hall et al. (eds.), *Culture, Media, Language* (pp. 128–138). London: Hutchinson.

Hall, S. (1996). The Problem of Ideology: Marxism Without Guarantees. In D. Morley & K. Chen (eds.), *Stuart Hall: Critical Dialogues in Cultural Studies* (pp. 25–46). New York: Routledge.

Henry J. Kaiser Family Foundation. (2005). Generation M: Media in the lives of 8–18 year olds. Menlo Park, CA.

Hettrick, S. (1995). "Lion King" to Video March 3. *The Hollywood Reporter*, 27–29.

Hobbs, R. (1996). Media literacy, media activism. *Telemedium, the Journal of Media Literacy*, 42(3), ii–iv.

Hobbs, R. (1998). The seven great debates in the media literacy movement. *Journal of Communication*, 48 (1), 16–32.

Honeycutt, K. (1995, March 28). Oscars Reward "Gump'-tion." *The Hollywood Reporter* 1, 6–7, 10, 13.

hooks, b. (1994). Ice Cube Culture. Outlaw Culture: Resisting Representations. New York: Routledge.

Jenkins, H. (2000). Lessons from Littleton: What congress doesn't want to hear about youth and media. *Independent School*, 59 (2), p. 24–32, 34.

Jhally, S. & Lewis, J. (1998). The struggle over media literacy. *Journal of Communication*, 48 (1), 109–120.

Jolson-Colburn, J. (1995, March 2). Grammy Buzz boosts Boyz. *The Hollywood Reporter*, p. 1, 5.

Kellner, D. (2003). Cultural Studies, Multiculturalism, and Media Culture. In G. Dines & J. M. Humez (eds.), *Gender, Race and Class in Media* (2nd ed., pp. 9–22). Thousand Oaks, CA: Sage. Lee's movie. (2006, February 18). <http://www.leesmovieinfo.net/wbotitle.php?t=240§ion=3&type=4>.

Lull, J. (1995). Hegemony. In G. Dines & J. M. Humez (eds.), *Gender, Race and Class in Media* (2nd ed., pp. 61–66). Thousand Oaks, CA: Sage.

Marx, K. (1971). Preface. *Critique of Political Economy*. London: Lawrence and Wishart.

Marx, K. & Engels, F. (1970). *The German Ideology*. London: Lawrence and Wishart.

Matchan, L. (1994, June 24). "Lion King": Too fierce for kids? Experts warn of violence in Disney's latest feature. *The Boston Globe*, p. 1.

McChesney, R. W. (1999). *Rich Media, Poor Democracy: Communication Politics in Dubious Times*. Urbana, IL: University of Illinois Press.

Newberger, C. (1994, June 27). Intolerance is the real message of the Lion King. *The Boston Globe*, 11 (col 1).

Palmer, J. (2000). Animating Cultural Politics: Disney, Race and Social Movements in the 1990s. Unpublished dissertation. University of Michigan.

Said, E. (1978). *Orientalism*. New York: Vintage Books.

Schor, J. B. (2004). *Born To Buy*. New York: Scribner.

Shanahan, J. & Morgan, M. (1999). *Origins. Cultivation Theory and Research* (pp. 1–19). Cambridge: Cambridge University Press.

Sun, C. (Producer). (2001). *Mickey Mouse Monopoly: Disney, Childhood and Corporate Power* [Video]. Amherst, MA: Media Education Foundation.

Sun, C. F. & Scharrer, E. (2004). Staying true to Disney: College students' resistance to criticism of The Little Mermaid. *Communication Review*, 7(1), 35–56.

Ward, A. R. (1996). The Lion King's mythic narrative. *Journal of Popular Film & Television*, 23(4), 171–178.

Wong. (1999). Deconstructing the Walt Disney Animation *The Lion King*: Its Ideology and the Perspective of Hong Kong Chinese, *Kinema* (2006, February 19). <http://www.kinema.uwaterloo.ca/wong991.htm>.

On the Topic
of Film and Education:
A Conversation
with bell hooks

BELL HOOKS AND KELVIN SHAWN SEALEY

As part of a series of public interviews held on the campus of Columbia University, I had the opportunity to speak to bell hooks about her cinema scholarship in November of 2004. On that day, in her trademark style, bell made a number of provocative statements about film and her many years of academic engagement with the cinema. Not having the time then and there to probe as deeply as I wanted into some of her comments, I took the opportunity to record another shorter private dialog I held with her two years later. The transcript from that conversation is printed below, and continues the theme found throughout this text relating to the potential for pedagogical engagement between cinema and its viewers.

—KELVIN SEALEY

Kelvin Sealey: Our conversation today will be for the final chapter in the book, *Film, Politics and Education*. I'm interested in looking at what could be called bell hooks' educational theory, your conceptualization of education, particularly from a Frieran perspective. What I'd like to throw into the mix is the extent to which cinematic images, or a set of cinematic images built into your educational theory, suggest a larger, more robust theory of pedagogy.

bell hooks: We have to start with the fact that my pedagogical theories, while influenced by Friere, are also deeply influenced by feminist thinking and practice.

KS: Please continue …

bh: Different from Camus. Even though he came [into it] late in life. It didn't really inform his earlier work.

KS: Okay—so, shouldn't we look at both your conceptualization of critical theory, then how feminist theory informs your educational theory, and then the extent to which a cinematic perspective might inform either of those or even a blend of the two? I'm not quite sure how to bring those three together, but let's do this as an experiment, since I want to believe that particularly with film, politics, and education, that critical pedagogy, that the cinematic, what I call cinematic education or pedagogy infused with the moving image, and feminist theory, can form a trio, a pedagogical trio, that allows us to use all three in a liberating way.

bh: My approach is more basic. I basically believe that media is the pedagogy of our times, and so because I feel like most of what people are learning about gender, race, class is coming from media and especially movies, to me movies become the perfect tool for film for teaching critical thinking and critical theories. Because people will, when you explain something to them just coldly, theoretically—a lot of times my students will say, well I don't get it. But if they watch a film and I begin to break down with them to deconstruct with them what's happening in the film, they see things completely differently, which is why film is one of the best tools for critical pedagogy. Because it allows people to, in a sense, have this space of consternation between what they think race, gender, class is all about and what perceived pedagogy is, and there is a challenge there. A good example is this recent film *Crash*. Where many people I talked to initially said, "This is a great film about race in America." And I would say, "Well how can you say this is a great film? Look at what it does with race, look at what it does with class." But also, when we really break down what it's doing with race, you know, it's almost a "Birth of a Nation" film, it's, it's the same old tropes. That we get who the hero is in the classical sense, but these are things that most people, I found, didn't see when they first look at the film. And so they began to ask those critical thinking questions—who, what, where, when, and why—suddenly they see a totally different film altogether.

KS: So when we consider film from an entertainment perspective, we're not as sensitized to the dimensions of power, of gender, of class that might imbue the film. But to the extent that a film is shown alongside a desire to build a critical pedagogy within the audience of students and perhaps the wider society, then we become more, then we begin to see with a critical pedagogical eye how a film might be used as a critical tool.

bh: Well, I don't accept the dichotomy between entertainment and awareness because I think one can be deeply entertained and fully critically aware. I don't think that the people who thought that *Crash* was a brilliant discussion of race actually thought they were being so much entertained as their awareness, their critical awareness, is so shallow as I think our nation has a very shallow, superficial understanding of race and white supremacy and how it works. So that it's, I mean part of what I'm always telling my students, because my students used to say to me, "You hate Spike Lee"—no, I actually find a lot of Spike Lee's work very compelling, but I'm critical of it in different ways, which doesn't mean that I'm not entertained by it, that I don't enjoy it. So I think partially the challenge in critical pedagogy, and moving beyond dualism, is that one doesn't accept that dualism entertainment. That there is some break between the entertainment, critical awareness of what we're seeing on the screen. Because one can simultaneously be very critically conscious as you're watching a film and at the same time be very entertained by it. Like *Kill Bill*, which I thought on so many levels was, in terms of critical awareness, I found reprehensible, but at the same time there was an aspect of pure enjoyment of the structure of the film. The beauty. The action.

KS: The aesthetics.

bh: The cinematography.

KS: Yeah, well, it almost sounds as if you believe it is possible to have a critical audience be entertained and that aspect of the entertainment that should be critiqued, the tropes and stereotypes, what one could say are reprehensible, are actually accepted as being reprehensible while still being entertaining. Does that not suggest that the critical audience can not only distinguish between what is entertaining and what is critical but dismisses what needs to be criticized? Or dismisses that portion and accepts that portion that needs to be internalized as entertainment? I'm not sure. How do we create that bifurcation?

bh: I think by not having a bifurcation. By not having a sense of a wholeness, just as in our daily lives we balance seemingly paradoxical situations, so that the critical eye also has that. You know, it's as if you're operating on two levels simultaneously, and I think that, in part, what I believe about critical consciousness, in a way critical consciousness teaches people how to operate on multiple levels at any given moment in time, so that one recognizes multiple intentionalities.

KS: Yes. How would a Frieran critical pedagogy of film aid the subject?

bh: Well, I mean, since I don't see myself as a Frieran, I don't feel like I could answer that. But what I have often imagined, for example. Let's take a group like unemployed black men.

KS: Okay ...

bh: I've thought to myself, I mean one of the things we know is that black men are swiftly becoming the most illiterate group in our nation. So I thought, well, one of the ways that we could teach critical literacy to black men is that, if we would use theaters, you know, normally closed down during the day, and show films, and talk about what's happening in those films, again on levels of, you know, the film itself, on levels of the relationship to you and how you live your life. What do you see, you know? Experiments conducted in Africa among people who were not highly literate, [suggested] that viewers saw a totally different film than people who were literate.

So, identify unemployed black men with low levels of literacy. You want to bring them into critical consciousness and critical literacy, to be able to look at what they are seeing, and know what they do see. Because I remember that one of the things that happened when we showed this [particular] film, people saw, the group of people watching it, was that people were very entertained by "the mouse." But [the researcher] didn't know what they were talking about and they had to look at the film over and over again to see that, indeed, evidently while this was being filmed, there was a mouse running around and that the visual gaze of a person who's not literate is very different from the gaze of somebody who is. So I think working initially with what is that gaze and see how you begin to enlarge the scope of that gaze. I think one could use... I think about Friere's work, it would be possible to use that, and in my case, since I would be much more interested in a larger model that would get at the issue of domination of, and gender and race and class combine all of them. Begin to look at that. How do they move from this narrow case to a fuller gaze? A narrow understanding of self to a fuller understanding of self.

KS: The suggestion being that a fuller gaze upon the self, with this population, staying with this population, a fuller understanding of self …

bh: With low levels of literacy.

KS: With low levels of literacy, would allow them to enter more fully into an understanding of reclaiming themselves?

bh: Well, and fundamental to both, I would use the phrase to talk about my work, "engaged pedagogy," as we begin to think critically. And I think that, part of that as we begin to think critically about our lives and we gain a critical consciousness, we are always in the process of becoming subjects. We think of that particular group of men, of black males we've identified as being very objectified by the culture and by the nation in their objectification. Then we would have to know that any beginning of critical consciousness is really, the beginning of critical consciousness is the beginning self-making and connecting self to a world beyond the self.

KS: Yes, I like that. Part of the pedagogy that we're considering is a reconceptualization of space, as well as a reconceptualization of how film can enter into the lives of people, helping to build the human subject.

I want to take a minute, though, and go in the direction of feminism, particularly with regard to film. In conversations we have had, you suggested that you stopped writing about film academically because you felt yourself confronting the same images, the same ideas, the same problems, the same tropes. At the same time it seems to me we're becoming an even more visual culture and that with DVDs and videos compounding the fact that on the small screen [tv], we're now seeing these images multiple times delivered in multiple modes. Only a few weeks ago Steve Jobs introduced the video ipod so people will be walking around with these things, they'll be fed to us almost continually. So, it does seem as though feminist intervention, in this, in this mediated, heavily mediated space, would have some value to women, young women, girls, attempting to free themselves from these images that we know they're consuming now in ever greater quantities.

bh: Well, I think in part that what I meant about not writing academically about film is that I felt that I was articulating the same, in a sense, the same frame dominator culture, how it structures itself in the end and that, in a way the process was the same for whatever film. If you would take the frame from how you would look at it. I would be writing through that same lens, and I guess what I've been struggling with is the possibility of a different language, a different articulation. I found myself, for example, struggling with the film *Capote*. I felt that there was a tremendous homophobia underlying the film, but I felt that I had or at least struggled with, articulated what I mean by that. Just in thinking of the political, does a film have any kind of political responsibility in the sense that having a film focusing on a gay male that never really names his gayness, but that only actually gives us the shadow side of his personality? So, we have a familiar cinematic portrayal of gayness, that of people pathologically narcissistic willing to go to, you know, extremes to wound others and yet, and it's so skillfully done because in a way by the refusal to have a narrative of gayness overt in the film, it seeks to make it seem like, underneath that. For everyone who comes in with the knowledge that he's gay, then that's like saying gay is evil, inherently depraved. You know, what is his lust, because, you know, there's also a way that the film is about lust, or this young man of color. You know, Perry who's defined as "Indian." The other. I mean it's all so you begin to think. I mean, I saw so many people who urged me to go see that film, it's really a film about a writer's process, one of the best things in the film is about being a writer, and again, complete erasure that we're not just talking about the portrait of a writer, but the particular portrait of a gay writer, at a very homophobic point in our nation's history.

All of that kind of gets erased, and so, made me want to go back to writing about film and to try to find a language that is more relevant to our times. Just as we're talking about how film has been changing, the modes of access have been changing, the language has to change to the earlier language writing about these issues as they pertain to film. And so I thought that I would only go back to writing if I could come up with a more useful language extended, because otherwise I felt that people would use these other paradigms and bring them to films that they see.

KS: How do you come up with a new language? I'm digging into that notion as I'm speaking to you—how do you build a new language—that extends the old but at the same time breaks from the old?

bh: This is something we get from the vernacular. People who are not schooled or are not highly literate, reshaping words and reshaping language every day. I mean, a real problem of the bourgeoisie decorum of academic writing and academic thinking is that we're often not able to break through and come up with terms that redefine or defamiliarize ourselves. For example, a term like "dissing," which defamiliarizes the concept of showing disdain or contempt. We have a much harder time I think in academic culture because we are taught certain kinds of jargons.

… with coming up with new ways to speak on what we're talking about, a new way. I even mean like me, I struggled with this, "How do I name this?" Well, how would I begin to talk about this unspoken reality of the film? You could say it's both, it's film that's presented, you know, just as Capote said he was writing the nonfiction novel from the kind that becomes a nonfiction fiction portrait of his own reality, functions both as a documentary but then also a, quote, "entertaining film." Or also it will go down, no doubt go down in history as the gay film.

KS: Let's push that notion of the vernacular just a bit farther because it creates an interesting intersection between high culture and low culture that the academy has often found problematic.

bh: Well, let me say, before you continue, that one of the reasons why I have focused on film, is precisely because of the way film is sought across class, all classes, and I identify film as a pedagogical site more than, say, books or certain forms of music. Because people, across class, especially through the amazing world of home video, watch films that may or may not, that at a certain point may or may not be the kind of films they would have gone to a movie certainly to see—that array of the working class and unemployed members of my family stumble across films that they can see at home, felt like they could go to a movie theater to see. So that I think that film on video, for example white people who don't know any black people, never been into the home of a black person, but can now bring that film to their own homes.

KS: I'm thinking of *Ray*, about the musician Ray Charles.

bh: *Ray* is a good example. You can bring that film, you can bring that right into your bedroom. You can bring those black people right into your bedroom. You would, you would keep away from the intimate structure of your life.

KS: Do you think that's an integration of space?

bh: I actually see that as a, no, as a new kind of colonialism. A way, the fact that you bring those images into your space that you also get to control.

You don't have to be part of a collective when you're sitting in the movie theatre, and I was trying to remember, even with *Crash*, some people told me that they were afraid to go see *Crash* in the movie theater because it might lead to riots or to, you know. And I was thinking about how, frankly, that rationalized fear that often arises when films have to deal with—I mean nobody talks about Kronenberg's *History of Violence*—oh maybe that will incite people in the film. So when I say, "White people can bring *Crash* into their bedrooms, in their dens, or wherever in their intimate spaces," recognize that because you can, if an image is uncomfortable to you, not be a collective part of that image. Part of why I still love to go to the movies when it is packed with people, is to have that collective sense of mutually watching something and mutual response gauge, like when people are laughing at a particular point and be able to respond.

So I think that that kind of recolonization of attempt at control of the image, it's also an attempt I think to keep alive the dominator culture hierarchy, in real life. In real life, all black people are not poor. In fact, a significant, a number of black people in our culture are very wealthy. You know, choose your films in such a way so that you can sort of teach people underneath, or you talk back to those films. In your homes, as friends tell me their relatives do where you can, you know, "Oh look at those niggers," or this is just how they are, so you can keep alive the white supremacy but it becomes a narrative, an internal narrative.

KS: Privately.

bh: Yeah, narrative that you have control over that you don't have to worry that you'll be overseen, overheard, interpreted.

KS: Exactly.

KS: Vernacular, especially as embraced by the academy; popular culture kept at arms length, which rises from masses, can inform and give vocabulary to have a global conversation.

bh: It is, in a sense, the democratic place of pedagogy. One of the reasons I latched on to film more than any other pedagogy is it's democratic nature. That is to say you don't have to be literate to see a film, but also it was my fundamental belief talking to people on street corners, that everyone that sees a film thinks something critically about it whether or not they are articulating to themselves what they think of it. The whole apparatus at work there is that people who read, who may know, but rarely read, may not bring to that written text, but may bring to that visual text.

KS: You're speaking to unintentional pedagogy, passive learning, because by and large film is passive.

bh: Oh, absolutely.

KS: But it's learning, it can be critical learning nonetheless.

bh: Or it can be a place that can seek one out for greater understanding. I oftentimes see people …

KS: Everyone that sees a film thinks something critically about it. There's a critical apparatus at work there.

bh: Race is always divided out over everything, which is why we switch in narrative. I think, for example, in my feminist theory class, getting them to analyze Katrina from a feminist standpoint. First, but it wasn't about gender, it was about race. Black. Well, two categories that are profoundly gendered but I especially took….

As we close I want to pen the thought that film is a pedagogical structure.

Well, don't you think it's a great meeting place in the academy where intellectuals, academics in the academy, share something with people not of their same class, their same educational background? We don't share the same neighborhoods or the same foods, we don't even share in the same kinds of, you know, day-to-day life practices often, but we have film, again, as a meeting place is why it's so powerful.

KS: Which is why I was going to say Kindergarten–12th Grade. There's also potentially great resonance for film as a pedagogy as well. But you still have an entrenched bureaucracy.

bh: I would say you have a very conservative bureaucracy when video was first popularized. All of a sudden TV screens appeared in …

KS: Classrooms.

bh: In the public school system, we thought, "OK, education is about to be completely recolonized," and then of course, most of those screens are empty most of the time.

KS: Exactly.

bh: They represent a threat to the planned lessons, the planned, directed mode of thinking. The Third grade teacher is directly the mode of thinking of someone seeing an image that disrupts the need for a conservative world view.

KS: bell, that's exactly the point I want to make: politics in the educational system.

bh: Let's focus on a recent film, a Christian film, I'm forgetting the name.

KS: You mean that Mel Gibson directed?

bh: Exactly. Now, here's a case that, I don't know if you're aware of this, black people—my mother, who's in her seventies, has not been to the cinema in twenty years, went to see that film.

KS: And …

bh: Went out of their houses, churches, all around the nation, black churches as well, buses with people to see that film. So that poignantly describes film as a site of pedagogy, that cuts across class, have all these elderly people, many of whom are on a fixed income, all around this nation that went and paid their little money to see this film. Why, I mean what was it at this film? There were other films with a Christian theme, that sort of radical reinscribing of Christianity with our government. Very much pushing the imperialism of Christianity. Here's a film that has this subversive, pedagogical edge because people allow it to. How does it go from being this little film in many ways to, you know, working-class poor blacks in churches being compelled to spend their money to see this film? So what it shows us is that everyday people, ministers, understand film to be an important site that whatever they believe would happen with the witnessing of that film, a nation, a recommitment to fundamentalist Christianity. They were able to make everyday people see film, a conservative narrative but, in fact, imagery.

It was blasphemy to witness and I just want us to call attention— somewhere, someone recognizes how powerful film is as a pedagogical tool. Because it's not as if the producers of that film went around saying, "Take your church." It shows, again, I guess what I think about a lot are, what are our pedagogies, what are our critical pedagogies that move beyond the academy that have their birth somewhere outside the academy, in fact return to us, galvanize us, to think more deeply. Because whatever, the pedagogy that began here, it began outside. It even began outside the film world so that it comes back to us. Think about, if this could happen, how can we have other films move people and motive people and transform people? How do we get that energy going and the place of again? One doesn't have to read and write adequately to see a film. Again, one doesn't have to read or write adequately to watch a film.

KS: No you make an excellent point. I'm not going to tax you here anymore here this morning. You've raised a number of points that I feel personally I need to follow up on—I don't know if you've raised some that you yourself want to follow up on, particularly with respect to films you've mentioned.

bh: I would just close by saying I'm very interested right now in how, in a sense, I would say, "Kelvin, more conservative forces acknowledge such a tremendous pedagogical possibility." That's why I think those of us who are progressive don't see using film as a means of sharing film as a way of sharing insight, pushing people to a higher, toward greater critical thinking, because I think there is a way in which the democratic nature of cinema and much of media actually makes intellectuals and academics look down on it like it's not really serious enough. In fact, it's that those conservatives that are saying, "Yes, it is." Just how powerful it is. We would do well as leftist people or people on the left, people concerned about the anti-intellectual, would do well to seek to recognize film as the site of multiple intentionality and possibility.

Contributors

Barry Bergdoll, Professor of Art History at Columbia University, is also the Philip Johnson Chief Curator of the Department of Architecture and Design at the Museum of Modern Art. He can be reached at barry_bergdoll@moma.org.

Annette Louise Bickford is an adjunct professor at the University of Toronto and can be reached at annette.bickford@utoronto.ca

John Broughton is Associate Professor of Psychology and Education and a founding director of the Film & Education Research Academy (FERA) at Teachers College, Columbia University. He can be reached at jmb61@columbia.edu.

Elizabeth Ellsworth is a Professor of Media Studies and Film, New School University. She can be reached at ellswore@newschool.edu.

Sun, Chyng Feng, a producer and filmmaker of numerous documentaries, is Master Teacher of Media Studies at the Paul McGhee Liberal Arts Division, School of Continuing and Professional Studies at New York University. She can be reached at cfs1@nyu.edu.

bell hooks is a Scholar in Residence at Berea College in Berea Kentucky.

Peter Lucas is Adjunct Professor of Photography & Imaging in the Department of Latin American and Caribbean Studies at New York University. He can be reached at Peterlucas@nyu.edu.

Kelvin Shawn Sealey, a visiting scholar and a founding director of the Film & Education Research Academy (FERA) at Teachers College, Columbia University, is the president of Instructional Effects, Inc., an educational consultancy. He can be reached at kss2008@columbia.edu.

Index